INSTANT SPEAKING SUCCESS

instant SPEAKING SUCCESS

Taking You From Dull to Dynamic

paul b. evans

Achievement Press
Montgomery, AL

Published by Achievement Press
Montgomery, AL

www.InstantSpeakingSuccess.com

Copyright © 2010 Paul B. Evans

Cover Art by Paul B. Evans

Cover Photos © 2010
www.RolandKrijnen.com

Cover Design and Interior Layout by Imagine! Studios™
www.artsimagine.com

All rights reserved. No part of this publication may be reproduced or transmitted in any form or by any means, including informational storage and retrieval systems, without permission in writing from the copyright holder, except for brief quotations in a review.

Quote used with permission of the Virginia Star Global Network www.satirglobal.org. All rights reserved.

Limits of Liability/Disclaimer of Warranty

The author and publisher of this book and the accompanying materials have used their best efforts in preparing this program. The author and publisher do not warrant the performance, effectiveness, or applicability of any sites listed in this book. All references are for informational purposes only and are not warranted for content, accuracy, or any other implied or explicit purposes.

This manual contains material protected under International and Federal Copyright Laws and Treaties. Any unauthorized reprint or use of this material is prohibited.

ISBN 13: 978-0-9831851-4-7

LCCN: 2011902110

First Achievement Press printing, February 2011

Dedication

To my wife Marla, who still thinks I'm funny and fresh at home or on the road.

I love you.

Instant Speaking Success is dedicated to all who have ever said a stuttering word from behind the large oak podium of a civic club luncheon.

Bless you!

TABLE OF CONTENTS

Dedication.. 5
More Than Words 9
The Course Condensed... 23
Step 1: PURPOSE.. 25
   Step One in Practice 38
Step 2: POINTS... 39
   Step Two in Practice 54
Step 3: PROOF.. 55
   Step Three in Practice 94
Step 4: POWER.. 97
   Step Four in Practice 119
Step 5: PASSION... 123
Step 6: PERIMETERS 129
Step 7: PRACTICE.. 137
Putting It All Together..................................... 145
Problem FREE Consultation................................... 155
Make Money without Speaking! 157
The Next Levels 159
About the Author 161

MORE THAN WORDS

"A speech is poetry: cadence, rhythm, imagery, sweep! A speech reminds us that words, like children, have power to make dance the dullest beanbag of a heart."

—Peggy Noonan

Words.

Words contain the power to alter the lives of mankind and of nations.

Words motivate, captivate, and infuriate.

Words create mental pictures that can produce desire or disgust.

Never underestimate the power of **your** words.

Sticks and stones can break my bones but words . . . words can break my spirit . . . or build my spirit . . . depending on how you use them.

Words, both written and spoken, influence.

This book will help you construct your words in a way that a group of people learns, laughs, and loves to hear you again. It contains what you need to design, develop, and deliver great speeches, messages, or whatever you want to call them.

But I want you to know three things . . .

1. Do not overcomplicate speaking. If you can carry on a conversation with another human being and keep his or her attention, you can speak publicly.

2. The book is easy to follow. The concepts presented are not only easy to follow, but they are also easy to master.

3. The principles you are about to study really work. These are the exact principles I use, whether I'm speaking to twenty or to more than two thousand. This is not hypothetical information.

Communicating Means

- Connecting on the heart level with the audience.
- Providing useful and relevant information that those present can imagine altering their lives for the good.
- Imprinting a thought on the mind so it cannot be forgotten (i.e., "I have a dream . . . ").
- Creating word pictures that allow attendees to live the moment with you.
- Making good use of the time so it is viewed as an investment rather than an expense.

Good communication has always appealed to our culture. We love to hear a great lesson or keynote speaker or seminar leader. We **want** to applaud. We **want** our lives to be changed from the rich information we receive, but . . .

Let's Face It . . . Some People Are Dull

They don't want to be. They **don't even know** they are boring. But they are.

Someone, somewhere, at some time said, "Hey why don't you teach this class?" Or, "How about giving an after-dinner talk at our club?"

That's how it started, and ever since they have been talking on and on and on, much to the regret of the audience.

No one has the heart to ask them to stop. And everyone else is too afraid to step up to the microphone for fear that they may become the next bearer of dry words.

That might sound harsh. It may not be proper to voice out loud, but it is true. And that's why you are reading this right now. You don't want to be that person. You don't want to be dull. You want people to smile when they hear that you will be speaking. You want people to anticipate and look forward to your presentation.

What Can Block Your Message?

Listening to a speaker whose good message is lost in poor techniques is like being given a precious diamond wrapped in burlap: You don't appreciate the value of the jewel because the presentation impedes your vision. You want your listeners to hear the heart of your message; you want your passion to show through. But how can you block your own good ideas and how can you allow your message to shine through?

Usually a combination of factors keeps your audience from truly hearing your message, but here are some of the most common.

A monotone voice

A voice that fails to vary in pitch will not only hides the value of your message, but it will also lull a crowd to sleep. As we communicate it's nice to imagine that what we have to say is of such value no one would dare miss a word. Unfortunately, that's only imagination; you must also take care to present the ideas with energy.

Lack of clear focus

No matter the audience, they all seek the same thing—life-changing information that can be applied immediately. Yet, we have all heard someone who talked for an hour and had nothing to say.

I once purchased a recording of a talk that promised "104 Ways to Boost Your Creativity." I eagerly anticipated listening to it, but didn't get quite the experience I was expecting. The presenter said, "I have a microphone positioned in the aisle. Let's use this period to let you share some creative ideas you have had." Not only was I disappointed at the lack of information. The speaker didn't speak, and the tape journeyed from point to point with no connection, no direction.

Rambling

Rambling is fine for tumbleweeds, but not communicators. These people go round and round, where they'll stop no one knows (Although everyone hopes they will stop, and soon!)

Ramblers tell stories not associated with the topic. One thing reminds him of another until even the speaker is lost. "Where was I" is a common phrase for the rambler. When coupled with a monotone voice this presenter can set a record for losing a crowd's attention.

Lack of facial expression

Deadpan, expressionless speakers bore us because many of us believe that our emotions should be worn not on our sleeves but on our faces. When someone we want to see enters the room, we smile. When a funny joke is told, we laugh. When our team scores, we cheer. All of these events are filled with expression.

A person who speaks and remains expressionless tells the audience that the subject is not interesting. She says by her appearance that the topic is not worth getting physically worked up over. He says by a lack of facial expression that the topic does not move him enough internally to move him externally.

No passion

Passion is contagious. A speaker who is excited about the subject can make even the least interesting topic engaging. Of course, the most exciting topic in the world can be reduced to a yawn with a passionless presenter.

I like to think of passion as *energy of the spirit*. It is internal electricity that lights up our bodies. When we have passion about a topic it shows. Others can't help noticing and being drawn into our excitement.

Failing to consider your audience

How much we like and care about a subject doesn't matter if our audience isn't interested. That does not mean that we can't take a subject that a group might think is dull and make it interesting. (*The Prayer of Jabez* sold millions of copies and it was taken out of a seemingly boring list of genealogies.)

However, as a preacher friend of mine learned, it is tough to keep a crowd through thirteen weeks of "Small Creatures of the Old Testament." As a speaker, your responsibility, your duty, is to understand your audience and their needs well enough to choose a topic that they will find timely, useful, and inspiring.

Slouchy appearance

How we look when we speak is important. A later section in this manual will cover personal appearance in more detail. For now it is enough to remind you that the first impression you make is nearly always visual, and that the more you can do to convey energy and enthusiasm for your subject the more likely your audience is to go along with you. Your energy, your posture, and your body language can begin to engage your listeners before you speak the first word. Your appearance should say that you care about yourself and the message you have to deliver.

Unvarying speech patterns

Slow talkers can put us to sleep, as can fast talkers. Our brains are designed for rapid assimilation of information, but we need sound cues to tell us when to pay attention. When details come in a sluggish rate our minds become bored. When they come at too rapid a rate, we tune out. There is not enough to keep the brain active in either case. Our brains shut down, causing us to fall asleep or daydream.

Stretching ten minutes of information into an hour

Some people follow the adage "Tell them what you are going to tell them. Tell them. Then tell them what you told them."

Others follow: "Tell them what you are going to tell them. Tell them. Tell them again . . . and again . . . and again . . . and again . . . and again . . . and again . . . and again." And by the time they get to the conclusion everyone has tuned out mentally.

If you only have twenty minutes of information, then only speak for twenty minutes. There is no reason to continue when nothing new or fresh is being presented.

Reading instead of speaking

Only the extremely talented can get away with reading their presentation. Combine reading with monotone, or an expressionless face, and you have a solid tranquilizer recipe.

The entire talk does not have to be memorized. A nice outline will serve you well. But a word-for-word manuscript read aloud will rarely be forgiven.

Insufficient eye contact

Eyes are the windows of the _____. (Did you put soul in the blank?)

We do not trust people who will not look at us in the eye. We think they are hiding something. When a child does something wrong we tell him to look us in the eye and tell the truth. We believe that we can look at the eyes and determine just how honest a person is being with us. It's the same when we speak. The audience weighs our words by our eyes. If they're shifty, they think we're shifty. If our eyes avoid contact, listeners think we are avoiding the truth.

Annoying physical habits

We all have something we do physically that is repetitive and potentially distracting. An audience—especially a young audience—picks up on these things. Do you know a speaker who seems to constantly push his glasses back up on his nose? A lady who slips her shoe on and off as she speaks? Someone who jingles his keys or change in his pockets? Someone who uses the same gesture pattern over and over?

These attributes not only divert our attention, they drive us crazy! Amazingly, most of these things could be alleviated if someone would speak up and tell us about our repetitive physical actions. However, since most people are a bit shy about telling us things that they think we don't want to hear, we often have to take the initiative to ask others what about our speech patterns distract them. It's a useful—and humbling—exercise.

What Turns You Off—And On?

Think about your least favorite speaker. What is it that disturbs you so much? What makes you unable to listen? What distracts you?

Whatever you listed, or whatever came to mind . . . don't do it. Be conscious of your communication skills and vow not to repeat the mistakes you have seen in others. Seek to develop techniques that will make you a successful communicator. Model yourself after good speakers you admire. You don't want to mimic them, but you can decide how to make their techniques useful to your style.

On the Other Hand

There are some people we would drive hours to hear. Every word greets our ears like music. Every thought is like honey to our hungry hearts.

They talk about topics you want to hear

The title alone may be enough to draw you in and want to attend. But whatever the subject is, you want to hear about it. You know it will change your life in some way. You know that you will be different, better, because of it.

Their voices draw you in

No, you don't have to have a perfect speaking voice, but there are certain voices that draw us. Maybe it's the caring tone, or the depth, or the confidence. Whatever it is, these people lack annoying vocal qualities that can be turn-offs and they have developed strong, clear, lively speaking voices.

Your personalities may be similar

A person that we like to hear often resembles our personal style. If we are humorous then we like to hear someone funny over someone dry. If we are more serious and reflective we like to listen to people with those same qualities. Now, while you can't be all things to all people, you can develop an ability to pay attention to your audience and connect with them on common points. Watch what they respond to and give them more when you see that they seem to enjoy some aspect of your manner — humor, empathy, excitement. Remembering that you're talking to people and checking in with them often can give great energy to your presentations.

Their points are relevant to your life

We want "walk-away" value. In other words we want to be able to exit the building with some knowledge or idea that can be useful to our lives right now. We want to be able to apply it on the spot. We want to see measurable differences when we apply the principles they discussed.

A speaker that can address our problems and present a solution captivates us. Everyone seems to be looking for the "secret" that will propel his or her life into bliss. The speaker that provides relevant points (secrets) will always bring in a crowd.

Their stories make you smile, or cry, or experience some other emotional response

Advertisers have taught for years that people "Buy on emotion, and justify with facts." In a presentation, the points are the facts and the illustrations are the emotion. The illustrations, stories, can bring home a point more powerfully than a list of true, yet sterile, facts.

A speaker who tells a great story not only keeps the attention of the crowd, but also connects with them. We believe and trust information that touches both our minds and our hearts more than that which only touches our minds.

Head stuff can seem cold, somewhat antiseptic. Someone who pours his or her message into our hearts causes us to learn and act.

They use props and other visual aids

A prop is anything that that can be used to illustrate a point in order to help the audience retain the message. Anything can be used: overheads, media forms, objects. The best communicators know how to use visual aids to add value and never to distract from the purpose.

They make you feel like you are the only one in the audience

Usually this is a combination of two things: eye contact and relevance.

Regarding eye contact, you cannot, of course, look at one person throughout the presentation, but you can connect through your eyes. When other people can see our eyes, we create a bond of likeability and trust.

As for relevance, when someone speaks about a subject that we are personally dealing with we feel that the speaker knows us. Somehow they were able to peer into our lives, witness our problems, and offer a solution.

They are real

Bill Hybels, pastor of Willow Creek Community Church, says, "People do not expect you to be perfect. They do expect you to be authentic."

Authenticity and genuineness are like magnets, while a person we perceive as phony repels us. Why? Because most people peg speakers as ego-bound. When a presenter who is humble and real steps forward, the contrast appeals to us.

They speak in conversational tones

With all crowds, but especially when you are teaching a younger group it is a must to *talk* to them. A conversational speaker attracts us much more than a formal, more detached, one.

Have you ever enjoyed talking with someone one-on-one only to find that this person's voice and behavior changed completely when he stepped up to the platform to speak? You want your speech from the podium to be just as real and confident as your speech from the next chair.

They talk to you, rather than down to you

I readily admit that I am not a genius, but that doesn't mean I want someone to make me feel inadequate or foolish. The best speakers compliment their audiences by talking on an educated level without using jargon or other terms that leave people feeling out of the loop.

Your Favorite Speaker

Write down the name of your favorite speaker:

_____

What does he or she do that you love so much?

_____

_____

What is different about that person than the average speaker you hear?

_____

_____

Which Brings Us to You!

You probably have a clear mental picture of what you do and do not want to be as a speaker. Maybe you have spoken for years and want to become more precise. Or perhaps you have a desire to teach but really don't know where to begin.

Begin by honestly looking at your strengths and weaknesses. What are your natural speaking strengths, areas in which you feel confident? List four or five.

_____

_____

_____

_____

Conversely, you need to know where you have room for improvement. Which aspects of great communication are not natural for you? Again, list four or five.

_____

_____

_____

_____

How can you work on sharpening those skills you already possess while working to hone new skills? That's what this book will help you to do.

Speaking of Goals

Write out the **perfect picture** you have in your mind of what a perfect speech or lesson would be.

_____

_____

_____

Describe audience's faces and body positions:

Attentive and open

What do you see in their eyes?

What will their reaction be at the end?

That they have gained something

What will they say to you as they exit?

Loved your talk, that was great. How do I work with you?

Steps to Crafting Unforgettable Messages

You should start with three simple goals:

1. Communicate with Purpose:

You never want to step in front of any group without a clearly carved purpose. Each effective talk has one. It is the narrowed subject. It is the one sentence you want every person to walk away with. It is the phrase that relates to every point, illustration or story.

Every speech needs to be able to be distilled into a single sentence that you can tell anyone at any time. It is the backbone of your talk and it will allow you to make every phrase count in your talk. Knowing this one focal point will make it easy to eliminate any elements of your talk that will not support it.

2. Communicate with Passion:

If nothing else, the people you present to must know that you believe in what you say.

Passion is energy of the spirit. It is what fuels us when we think we cannot continue. This energy source forces us to share our message because we know we will be incomplete if we don't. Passion says that others will be incomplete if they do not hear the message within us.

Passion is contagious. Not only does passion fuel us, it fuels others. Haven't you been around someone who was so excited that before you knew it you were excited, too? When you learn to communicate with passion, others will not only believe what you say, they will feel what you feel, and will be compelled to do what you do.

3. Communicate with Precision:

A talk can be like throwing grain to the hens, or it can be like a laser during eye surgery. If you throw grain, the hens will get stuffed, but there is a great deal of waste as well. If your message is like a laser it will waste no effort and everyone will leave with clear vision.

So let's get to it. You are about to learn how to forge an unforgettable message even if the crowd doesn't take notes.

THE COURSE CONDENSED

Here's what you are about to discover. I'll take you step-by-step through the process.

Step 1: Purpose

You must be able to summarize your message in one sentence. It is the concept you want the audience to leave with even if they forget all else.

Step 2. Points

Your points tie directly to your purpose. They support the premise of the talk and provide ways to make the purpose real in the lives of the listeners.

Step 3: Proof

Every illustration, statistic, and quotation provides proof of the points you make. It helps make the point memorable and ultimately leads back to the purpose of the entire speech.

Step 4: Power

The opening and closing of the message are critical. They determine if you will gain attention at the beginning and determine if you will be invited back at the end.

Step 5: Perimeters

The perimeter refers to the outside edge of an area. I will use this term to refer to externals of your speaking, areas that can easily consume us—voice, attire, gestures.

Step 6: Practice

You don't need to memorize the message to do a great job, but you do need confidence and that comes from practice. This section will help you get the most from your preparation.

Step 7: Passion

If you don't have this, you don't have much. Raise the "oomph" of the room through your zeal.

Step 1
PURPOSE

"Make sure you have finished speaking before your audience has finished listening."

\- Dorothy Sarnoff

Speaking Myths

Myth #1: "I've got to be the best."

I used to live by this myth. My mind would tell me to forget about speaking. If I couldn't be the best, there was no use stepping on stage. But that changed. I decided to take a slightly different approach. Instead of being the best, I wanted to focus on improvement. I knew that every event, every speaking engagement, offered me the opportunity to improve over my last attempt. When I stopped competing against an ideal and worked instead toward a goal of honing my strengths and overcoming my weaknesses, I wasn't so daunted by speaking. I began to enjoy the process.

The truth is that you only have to be the best you that you can be. Don't fall into the speaker trap of thinking more about yourself than about your audience.

Myth #1 comes into play when your thoughts are "I hope they like me," "I hope I don't mess up," or "I hope I don't freeze."

Are any of those phrases about the audience?

Myth #2: "I've got no business speaking to this group. I'm not an expert on anything."

Wrong. You're an expert on your experiences and interpretations of life. Go to the bookstore and browse. There are thousands of people making millions of dollars based on **their opinions**. They simply know how to communicate their personal know-how.

The **ONLY** thing you **HAVE** to do is have a definite purpose for your message and allow everything you say to support it.

The Reason I've Called You Here

No matter whom you are speaking to or for, you must have purpose. There must be a *distinct reason* for you to stand before a crowd.

Your purpose is the ONE concept you want to communicate—one phrase, one sentence—that sums up the talk. Decide what is the one idea that you want the audience to remember even if they forget all else.

Remember that your audience wants to

- Know that they will be changed for the better for having listened to you; they want something that will alter their lives.

- Gain information that will enable them to make it through the next day with success.
- Know that they are not wasting their time.
- Believe that if they miss your message they could miss something major.
- Know that what you present is relevant and applicable.
- Be confident that the talk will be entertaining and engaging.
- Learn something they didn't know.
- Be affirmed in something they did know.

According to Tony Jeary, author of *Inspire Any Audience*, people want to belong, to be respected, to be liked, to be safe, to succeed, to find romance, to be inspired. While your talk can't fulfill all of their dreams, you may be able to help unlock some of the things that have been blocking them, simply by sharing your own experiences honestly. That is the power of speaking with true purpose. A successful speaker is able to plug into these basic human desires through the content in his or her message and hammer it home with points and proof.

Irrefutable Law of Speaking:

*If You Don't Know the Purpose of the Message,
You Can't Expect the Audience To Gain Any Specific Value.*

On an elementary level there are four possible purposes of any speech: to inform, instruct, persuade, or entertain. Those are basic concepts that anyone can accomplish. You need to pursue the purpose of your talk on a deeper level.

Your purpose will be communicated through the topic, the audience, and the intended outcome.

Five Ways To Choose Your Topic

1: The Call To Speak

This is the majority of beginning speakers. You've been **told** that you're going to speak. The boss says you're the one, so you are on deck. Maybe your service club, church, or other organization wants you to give a talk at a meeting. The tough thing about being told to speak is that it often comes with a generic subject: "Just get up and share a little bit." This can be intimidating, but it's actually a wonderful opportunity. The invitation comes to you because those asking believe that you have something beneficial to share. So begin by looking at your life and seeing what unique experiences you have that can be of value.

2: Your Passion

Do you have an internal fire to get your message out? Maybe you want to speak about a political issue, or how to get over anxiety, or how to lose weight, or how to close more sales. Is there a topic that you feel you **must** speak about?

3: Your Knowledge

Do you possess some specialized information that others could benefit from knowing? Are you an expert in a field?

4: Your Know-How

People love to learn from another's experience, especially if it will save them time and trouble. Don't sell yourself short on this issue. It is your greatest resource for topics. You might think you are not interesting, or that you are not special—this is not true. Each person's experience is unique and has the ability to teach another. It can literally be *any subject* that you have experienced and others will learn from. For example: If you have bought a car you could go to a dealership and share your pleasant or unpleasant experience in a talk designed to help the sales force improve their technique.

5: A Desire To Learn More

There may be a subject that you would like to know more about. Study and research the subject, then take your findings and design a talk.

Your Audience:

Of course, an essential part of crafting your message is taking the time to understand your audience and what they want and need. There are some important areas to consider about your audience; however, be careful not to overanalyze. If you are speaking locally, you probably know your audience well. When you begin to travel, it becomes more important to try to understand your audience in more detail.

Among the things you want to try to find out about your audience, if possible, are some basic demographics, for example age, sex, economic status, educational level, ethnicity, religion, political leanings, occupation, and other cultural issues that may affect how they respond to your message. You wouldn't give a talk on cooking the perfect steak to a group of vegetarians.

You may also want to consider character as you are determining the most appropriate message for your given audience. What values do they hold? How do they feel about the topic you are presenting and can you show them another side of the issue that they might not have considered? Are they deeply religious?

What attitudes and beliefs do you share and where do you diverge? Are there any stereotypes that could be harmful and how will you address them? How much do they know about your subject and can you show them a different aspect of it? Are they familiar with you and how will familiarity—or lack of familiarity—work in your favor? What do they expect and how can you surprise them?

Avoid the temptation to get too bogged down in the audience, however. Keep it simple. Some coaches will tell you that you need to know the break down of the audience to the *n*th degree. Not true. You generally need just a basic understanding of the top line issues important to your crowd unless you are speaking to a target industry or group.

Sometimes it is just as important that you know how to not to offend the audience as it is for you to know how to please them. Know what risks you can take and what is appropriate and inappropriate. For example, when I speak to a group of teenagers I'm much less formal than when I am speaking to a group of business people. My humor is different with each group.

It's also important to remember the 2/96/2 rule. If you give a clear, thoughtful speech, 2 percent of the audience will think you are the best speaker they ever heard. Another 2 percent will think you are the worst speaker they ever heard. Do not place too much value in either of these opinions. Rely instead on the 96 percent who will give you legitimate feedback and who will, over time, help you to become a more effective speaker.

And remember of course that the audience wants you to succeed! No one enters a meeting saying, "I hope this speaker stinks. I love being bored." Except for a few deranged members of the crowd, the vast majority wants you to make it.

The Pre-Event Questionnaire

Would you like to read the audience's mind and guarantee that you hit the major concerns of the people? One way to ensure that your message hits home is to send a pre-event questionnaire to your contact. Highlight the questions you need answered and leave the rest optional. This feedback will help you build a speech that is tailored to your audience.

Step 1: PURPOSE

Here is the questionnaire I used when I first got started. Feel free to rewrite it for your needs.

EVANS Communication & Consulting

Bull's Eye Speaking... Zero Zzzzzzzz's Guaranteed!

Pre-Program Questionnaire

3205 Little John Dr. Montgomery, AL 36109   334-549-4001
Paul@InstantSpeakingSuccess.com

Please Return Immediately

This questionnaire is designed to help us prepare a program specifically suited to the needs of your group. Please take a few minutes to fully answer all the questions and return the form to our office. Thanks for your help!

Special Request. If you feel that your company materials will help in preparation, please send them as well.

1. How did you hear about Paul Evans? _____
2. Event type: (Annual meeting, Convention, etc) _____
3. Proper attire for speaker (Please check one) ____Business Suit ____Black Tie ____Business Casual
4. Meeting Theme: _____
5. Contact Person _____ Email/Phone _____
6. What take's place immediately before Paul's presentation?_____
7. What do you consider the primary strengths of your organization?
    A _____
    B _____
    C _____
8. What are the top 3 challenges faced by the member's of your group?
    A _____
    B _____
    C _____
9. What are the approximate characteristics of your average member?
    A Age _____ B. Sex _____ C. Income level_____ Education _____
10. How many people, approximately, will be in the audience? _____
11. What 3 things do you think we should know about your group? (stereotypes, jargon, dreams)
    A _____
    B _____
    C _____
12. What professional speakers have you used in the past and what did they discuss?
    A _____
    B _____
    C _____

Pre-Program Questionnaire Page 2

EVANS Communication & Consulting
Bull's Eye Speaking... Zero Zzzzzzzz's Guaranteed!

3205 Little John Dr. Montgomery, AL 36109   334-549-4001
Paul@InstantSpeakingSuccess.com

13. What are the 3 most significant events that have taken place in your industry in the past year?

   A. _____
   B. _____
   C. _____

Critical Questions:

14. Specifically, what do you want to accomplish in this session? _____
_____
_____

15. What are your objective overall with the event? _____
_____
_____

16. Are there any key issues or topics that you feel need to be addressed? _____
_____
_____

17. Names and numbers of 4 people Paul can contact who will be in attendance to increase the value of the program:

A. _____ Phone _____ B. _____ Phone _____
C. _____ Phone _____ D. _____ Phone _____

18. Do you have any other suggestions to help make this your most successful program ever?
_____
_____
_____
_____
_____
_____

Step 1: PURPOSE

The Ultimate Outcome

When the meeting or event is over what do you want the audience to leave with? What concept? What idea? What unforgettable belief? What new opinion? What information?

Your **Purpose** is the Bull's-eye of the message, the target you want to hit. You may have noticed that a Bull's-eye is part of my Evans Communication and Consulting logo. My tagline is "Bull's-eye speaking . . . Zero Zzzzzzzzs Guaranteed." You can tell I'm serious about the outcome of my presentations.

After you select your topic, and you know your audience, you're ready to move into **the formula for Bull's-eye success**.

Narrow Topic + Head + Heart = Bull's-Eye Speaking

Narrow Topic

Make It Clear and Precise

The message needs to have pinpoint accuracy. General topics will have general outcomes. No one will know what you talked about. You can even tell a lot of jokes and get the crowd going, but if you don't share something targeted they might leave saying, "Well that was entertaining, but I don't have a clue what the message was about."

Again, ask yourself what is the one thing you want your audience to leave with?

Throughout this book we'll build a talk on goals. So let's begin right now as we learn to narrow our topic.

First, "goals" is a broad topic. There's too much information on the subject. You could speak for days on the various aspects.

Some goal ideas...

- Goal setting
- Goal attaining
- Getting started
- Long-term goals
- Short-term goals
- Lifelong goals

Any of those could be a speech. But even then they may not be narrow enough to create specific rather than general understanding of your subject.

You can narrow further by adding a *narrowing phrase*.

- Goal setting for financial security
- Goal attaining for self-esteem
- Getting started—your first hour of goal planning
- Long-term goals for a secure retirement
- Short-term goals for becoming a vegetarian
- Lifelong goals for physical health

Make your topic as tight as possible.

Head

What do you want the people to think?

Next determine how you want to affect your audience's heads. What do you want to happen to them intellectually? How do you want to challenge them mentally?

Do you want to create awareness? Do you want to inform? Do you want to generate doubt?

Force the audience to think.

Heart

What do you want the audience to feel?

You want to impact their hearts. Do you want them to feel sad about the number of drunk driving accidents, or perhaps infuriated? Do you want the audience to feel joyful or electric after your talk? Maybe you want them to feel challenged, or uplifted, or light, or heavy?

Write down how you want them to feel after your talk.

For our goal speech here's how I laid it out:

Narrow topic: Goal Achievement for Life

+

Head: "The audience should compare where they are to where they could be."

+

Heart: "The audience should feel a belief in themselves and a hope for what can be accomplished."

Your Purpose Defined...

Your narrow topic: *The Impact of Poor Body Confidence on your business*

+

Head: *They should realise what beliefs they hold that may cost them clients*

+

Heart: *They should feel the need to change their beliefs in order to build their business.*

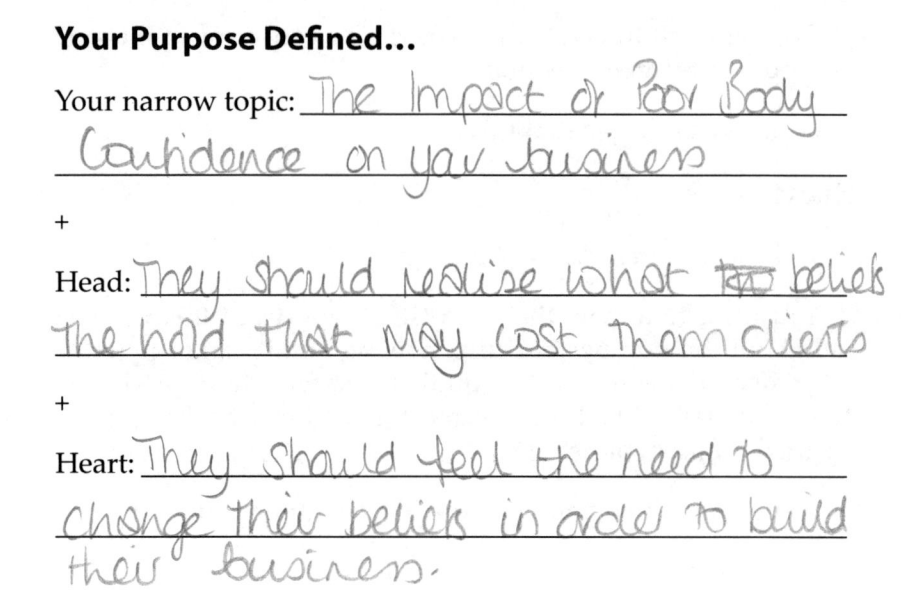

Irrefutable Law of Speaking

Engage Your Audience Intellectually and Emotionally.

The first step in drawing people to your purpose is through your talk's title.

Titles That Pull

A title works like a magnet. It either draws people or repels them. Create a good one and you have people wanting to hear you before you even step to the platform.

Benefits: a title that predicts a specific gain.

- How Our Department Gained 25 Percent in the Past Twelve Months and How Yours Can Too

Solutions: a title that promises an answer to a problem.

- Barely Breaking Even? Boost Your Profits by 25 Percent in Twelve Months

Curiosity: a title that raises questions.

- 25 Percent and Climbing

Rapport: a title that makes people feel accepted.

- We Did It and So Can You

Shocker: a title that creates surprise, scandal, or skepticism.

- What the Boss Doesn't Want You To Know

Teaser: a title that begs people to peek behind the curtain.

- Three Keys to Instant Increased Profits

Guarantee: a title that pledges satisfaction.

- More Profitable Ideas in One Hour or I'll Buy Your Lunch

Instant Titles

If you're having a tough time coming up with a title for your talks feel free just to fill in some blanks.

- _____ Ways To Become _____

- How I Went from _____ to _____ in Only _____

- The Little Known Secret of _____

- The Truth about _____

- Simple Techniques for _____

- An Easy 3 Step System to _____

- How To Avoid _____

- The ABCs of _____

- Why Almost Everyone Is Wrong about _____

- How To Turn _____ into _____

- Quick and Easy _____

- End Your _____

- _____ Ways to Bullet-Proof Your _____

Step One in Practice

Topic: Goal Achievement

Title: The Awesome Power of Goal Achieving

Purpose: "The audience should compare where they are to where they could be {head}, and should feel a belief in themselves and a hope for what can be accomplished {heart}."

Step 2
POINTS

"Be sincere; be brief; be seated."

—Franklin D. Roosevelt,
advice on speechmaking to his son James.

PURPOSE
↑
POINTS

Every point must lead back to the purpose. It must fulfill the objective for standing before the audience.

Irrefutable Law of Speaking
Points Must Be Clear, Precise, Meaningful, and Fun!

Points bring the purpose to life and explain it. While the purpose is the skeleton, the points are the flesh. Points give shape to the message.

How Many Points?

The amount of time you have determines the number of points you are going to present and how long each point will last.

Option 1: Time Based

I loosely arrange time like this:

- 30 minutes, 3 points, 8 minutes per point, 3 minute opener, 3 minute close.

- 60 Minutes, 6 points, 8 minutes per point, 8 minute opener, 4 minute close.

- 90 Minutes, 8 points, 10 minutes per point, 7 minute opener, 3 minute close.

Of course every point's timing isn't exact. If you expect it to be you're doomed. Do not memorize your message to the point of being inflexible. It's always fine to end early. Just don't go long (more on this later).

Option 2: Volume Based

Design your message with a great number of points. Like, "25 Tips for Great Goals," "Top Ten Goal Strategies," or "The 11 Secrets of Successful Goals."

Two ideas to consider: First, an advantage of having a lot of points is you have a wealth of material to cover. Second, you will be able to adjust your points and time at will. When time dwindles you can either cut points or go through the remaining ones at an even pace. However, don't simply rush to get through. As long as the audience does not know how many you planned to share, you can use five, ten, or more. If you only have time for three, then they will think you only planned to share three.

Option 3: The Rule of Three

The Rule of Three is used quite a bit in humor. You'll notice that in a joke the punch line often comes on the third involvement.

- Three men stood at the gate of heaven . . .
- Three little boys sat in class . . .
- Three blondes . . .

Three works because it triggers simple involvement. Fewer than three doesn't seem worth the effort and more than five gets tough to remember.

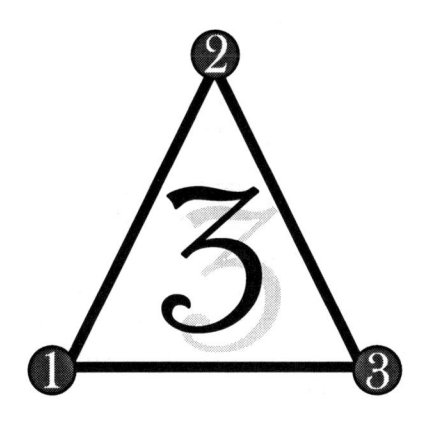

When you think of three, think symmetry. From the above, you can sense how easy it would be to connect all three points to a middle anchor (purpose).

The lower number helps your audience follow your talk easily and remember what you say. Once you get to six or more you need to tell the audience to take notes. Most will be unable to remember much more than five. Even in a balanced depiction like the one below you can tell that six points connected to an anchor would be a challenge to keep up with.

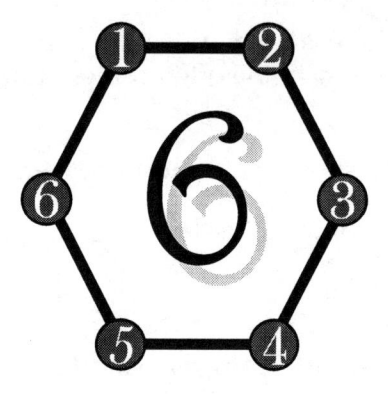

When in doubt about the number of points, three is always good as long as your talk isn't more than forty minutes. The symmetry creates rhythm.

Where Do I Find Material?

Once you have your purpose and you know how long you're going to talk, it's time to go out and gather information. And if there is anything that is available in mass, it's information. Your job is to take this information and present it to your audience in an organized and memorable manner. Unless you are presenting a speech that requires laboratory testing you can generally find enough on the Internet to cover any subject. So let's begin there.

Top Five Information Resources:

1. The Internet

Google, Dogpile, and Yahoo! are among the most popular and most usable search engines. You can also try Bing and Ask.com, which help your categorize and refine your search. Search Engine Watch.com also gives a comprehensive listing of some of the most popular search engines and directories.

Some other good resources for search that go beyond the basic norm include Resource Shelf, which allows researchers to share their finds; Complete Planet (aip.completeplanet.com) for deep Web searching of more than 70,000 databases; and MSN Search with easy settings for advanced search.

And do keep in mind that the Internet is a useful tool, but you have to be a careful researcher. Evaluate what you find and try to verify your facts by checking them against various sources. A useful tool to aid you in evaluating what you come across in search is the Snopes site, which helps you to steer clear of urban legends and false reports.

The Cornell University Library suggests that you consider five basic criteria in evaluating the usefulness of any site:

1. **Accuracy** – Does your page list the author and institution that published the page and provide a way of contacting him or her?

2. **Authority** – Does your page list the author's credentials and is its domain preferred (.edu, .gov, .org, or .net)?

3. **Objectivity** – Does your page provide accurate information with limited advertising and is it objective in presenting the information?

4. **Currency** – Is your page current and updated regularly (as stated on the page) and are the links (if any) are also up-to-date?

5. **Coverage** – Can you view the information properly — without paying fees or acquiring specific browser technology or additional software?

If you plan on using information from any source on the Internet or elsewhere, be sure to give credit to the source. For example: The Instant Speaking Success Letter. It wouldn't bother me if someone e-mailed and said, "Hey, I've got to do a talk on public speaking tonight. Would you mind if I shared your ten tips as long as I give you credit?" I'd be glad to have them do it, and the person would have an entire talk in less than thirty seconds. All they would need to add is an opening and closing, and practice a couple of times.

The Internet is how I conduct 98 percent of my research. Among the benefits is the fact that I get to stay home and find it quick.

2. The Library

You don't want to neglect the benefits of researching with real books and other resources that the public library offers. I especially like to use the library for current newspapers and magazines. And if you live in a city with a major university, the university library provides you access to a wealth of resources not available to the average speaker.

Use the librarian. The librarian is not only acquainted with most of the books the library contains, he or she is also familiar with the library's organization. That's the best option because the librarian can find in moments what might take you hours.

3. Your Life

People ask me if I brainstorm. I tell them my brain is a storm! You might have enough information stored away to fill in a four-point outline with little effort. Write down about twenty things that come to mind, and then choose four. Don't over complicate the process. The audience doesn't know if it took you two minutes or two years to develop the points. As long as it's valuable they won't care how long it took.

Don't sell yourself short here. You have a lot to offer others. Your unique perspective on a situation offers enough reason for you to be able to share it with those who may learn from it.

Actually, you are the most valuable resource in your arsenal. People will think it's nice that you were able to research a topic and form a speech. They will be much more tuned in if you share from your life.

Honestly, would you rather hear a speaker talk about, "Four Ways to Overcome Depression," or "How I Overcame the Darkest Depression and You Can Too"?

Humbly put yourself in the message.

4. Interviews

Maybe there's someone you know that the audience respects. This automatically lends credibility to yourself and your topic.

Example: You are asked to speak about the future of computer technology. You just happen to know Bill Gates, so you call him and get his input. Can you imagine stepping before the crowd and saying, "I was asked to present on the future of computer technology. I have a friend that knows a little something about computer technology. I called him this afternoon, and I want to share with you tonight what Bill Gates calls 'The Five Breakout Technologies of the Future.'" You wouldn't be able to pay people to leave the room.

To conduct a good interview you want to craft your questions to make the most of your interviewee's expertise. Ask his or her opinion on your topic and get insight on how the topic applies to your particular audience. How can you offer an insider's view? You want to get information that can't be found online or in a book or article. The real-world experience of your interview subject is valuable and will go a long way to making your message unique and powerful for your listeners.

Let the person you want to interview know you won't take much time and you'll only ask three to five questions. More on this technique later.

5. Bookstores

Barnes & Noble (which has great reading furniture) and Books-A-Million are great places to do some browsing. Large chain bookstores like these contain the newest books, conveniently arranged by subject. What a resource! In a matter of minutes you can find ten books on your topic and evaluate which ones will be the most useful to develop your talk. Booksellers can also help you find other books—as well as magazines and journals—that might relate to your topic and you can begin to build a library of current resources.

A Filing System?

The way you organize the information you collect is personal preference. If you're more systematic, you might want to create a system of labeled manila folders and place articles, quotes, and other materials in separate folders according to a category.

If you're less structured, you might use the yellow legal pad or notebook.

When I'm reading through books, I use a yellow legal pad and make notes of what I find. I write down the points I think will be useful, along with the reference information (book, author, page number).

When working online, I highlight the information and print that section. I then punch three holes in the printouts and put them in a binder. This is helpful, because the URL of the site, along with the date I found it, will be printed at the bottom of each page. I make sure to jot down any other relevant information (the name of the researcher, the sponsor of the study, the creator of the site), so that I can be sure to give proper credit. I collect all the information I possibly can on the topic and purpose of the message.

What Do I Do with All This Information?

The difficult part of gathering information is deciding how to use it all to organize and inform your talk.

Use only what supports your purpose. No matter how intriguing or beautifully worded the information or quotation might be, don't use it unless it points directly to the purpose.

After tossing the extraneous material, think about the points you want to make. If you find that almost every resource you uncovered mentions the same idea or concept then you definitely want to include it in your talk.

What points can you discover in the materials?

OPTION 1: Repeating Concepts

If you researched twenty sources you could probably list a minimum of forty points to talk about. But maybe you only need three to five.

First, make a master list. Write down every conceivable point that could be made from the sources you have before you. If several sources cover the same point, go ahead and write it down again. It doesn't matter if more than a hundred items make the list. Beside each point, record where it came from so you will be able to find it quickly.

Second, look through the list you developed and place and place an "X" by the points that were repeated more than once. This shows that it is a concept or idea that is popular and held as a common belief.

Third, determine the strongest points among those that repeat. Keep four or five to use in your talk—or as many as you need.

OPTION 2: The Road Less Traveled

Take the position of a contrarian.

First, make a master list as described above.

Second, immediately cross off the list any repeated concept.

Third, of the remaining ideas, which are the most outlandish, the least likely to be accepted by the mainstream?

A contrarian presentation can be extremely powerful and memorable. It will challenge and possibly infuriate the crowd, so be careful. To use a contrarian style of speaking you must have unquestionable proof, unshakable confidence, and unwavering commitment to your message.

Here's my **Option 1: Repeating Concepts** boiled down. Since we're building a talk on "The Awesome Power of Goal Achieving," I researched goals on the Internet. Here are the four concepts that kept repeating themselves. Plus a final point that I feel convicted about from personal experience.

1. Write Down Your Goals Specifically.
2. Set a Completion Date.
3. Map an Action Plan.
4. Use Daily Disciplines for Focus.
5. Assess Life Value Outcomes.

There were more than fifty ideas that I gathered from the various sources, but since the above existed in multiple Websites they contained the most strength and worth.

A quick word about using what you find. The above information is generic. If a person sat down and thought about it for a short period of time, he or she would probably come up with the same ideas on their own.

However, if a scientist or research company spent millions proving that "Setting a Completion Date" increases performance by 45.3 percent, then you must give the researcher credit. And you cannot use the information for moneymaking purposes without permission.

Now that we have our five points it's time to put them in a format that will help the audience remember and apply them.

How Do I Arrange the Points?

If you present the points the way you write them down originally that's fine. Look at the five points above. They're not bad, but they can be better. They can be more memorable.

Try to make the points so clear, that a year later a person could see you on the street and repeat them to you. Also, make it apparent that a pattern exists in your outline.

Here are five formats to choose from when structuring your material.

1. Acrostics:

This is a series of phrases where the first letter in each line can be combined to form a word. Here's an example from our points above.

"I want to share with you the secrets of achieving G.O.A.L.S."

- **G**et Specific
- **O**fficial Date
- **A**ction Plan
- **L**earn Discipline
- **S**ignificance

Those are the same concepts as listed originally, but they spell the word GOALS. Each letter will automatically connect the audience with the point you are making. It works like mental glue.

2. Alpha-Series:

Use sequential letters of the alphabet to make your points stick.

- **A**lways be Specific
- **B**ook Your Finish
- **C**reate a Plan
- **D**aily Discipline
- **E**levate Your Life

Or you could try another variation on the Alpha-Series.

- **A**lways be Specific
- **A**ppoint a Deadline
- **A**ctivate a Plan
- **A**pply Discipline
- **A**dvance Your Life

3. Rhyme

This is not my favorite. Yet it may be helpful in some situations, especially if you speak to children.

- *Rise* (Rise to a specific level of expectation)

- *Eyes* (See yourself completing the goal on a specific date)
- *Sky's* (The sky's the limit when you plan)
- *Prize* (You'll gain your prize when you stay focused and disciplined)
- *Size* (Your life will expand in positive ways)

4. Phrases:

Arrange your points so the first four or five words repeat at the beginning of each point.

- The Awesome Power of a Specific Desire
- The Awesome Power of a Specific Date
- The Awesome Power of a Specific Plan
- The Awesome Power of a Specific Focus
- The Awesome Power of a Specific Transformation

5. Analogies:

Tie the message to something the group is already familiar with.

"As I share with you about *The Awesome Power of Goal Achievement* I want you to consider the Super Bowl. Consider all the time and effort required to reach that level."

Here are the five points in analogy form:

- "*Set* a specific goal. That's what a championship team does."
- "Decide on a completion date and make it your *signal*. Every NFL player knows the date of the Bowl."

- "Create a *solid* plan. No coach practices for a championship by adlib."

- "Follow a *strict*, disciplined regimen to stay on course. Ask any professional player and he'll tell you the daily requirements of the sport."

- "Set goals that deliver *significant* life change. When a player wears a championship ring, it represents much more than winning one game."

At the end of the talk you could run back through the "S" scheme that runs through the points:

- Set.
- Signal.
- Solid.
- Strict.
- Significant.

Which Structure Is Best?

Consider the Audience

Simply think about the people in the seats. That's the most important aspect. It really doesn't matter if you are not thrilled with the format if the audience loves it.

There have been dozens of times when the message I brought and the outline I used were not my favorite choices, but people raved. Why? Because it was what they wanted. Remember that your focus as a speaker is to see that the audience receives value.

Consider the Subject

Of the above examples the rhyme scheme is the one that resonates the least with me personally. To my thinking, the subject is too serious for most people to use a rhyme. If a person has a tough time getting on track a rhyme will not help them take the action seriously. However, a group of elementary age children would love the rhyme.

Will the topic bear the format? Do they match? Do they complement each other? This is really more about a gut feeling and common sense. If you're still unsure, call the person who booked you and cover your outline. Ask for that person's input. This will not only make you more valuable as a speaker, but your contacts will feel that they have contributed to the occasion.

Consider the Occasion

A corporate event is approached differently than a civic club meeting. A church presentation calls for one format, while a high school lecture will call for another arrangement.

Regardless of the setting, or the audience, make your message unforgettable!

Irrefutable Law of Speaking

The BEST Structure Is the One YOU Are Most Confident Using.

Speaking gurus will tell you that it's all about the audience, and every decision should be based on them. So why do I tell you that the best structure is the one you are most confident using? Isn't that about you and not the audience?

Nope.

Being at your best *is* best for the audience. It's fine to break the rules as long as your purpose is clear—as long as you seek the attendees' highest value.

Step Two in Practice

Topic: Goal Achieving.

Title: The Awesome Power of Goal Achieving

Purpose: Learn how to achieve goals, not just set them.

Points:

- Write Down Your Goals Specifically.
- Set a Completion Date.
- Map an Action Plan.
- Use Daily Disciplines for Focus.
- Assess Life Value Outcomes

Points with Structure:

- The Awesome Power of a Specific Desire
- The Awesome Power of a Specific Date
- The Awesome Power of a Specific Plan
- The Awesome Power of a Specific Focus
- The Awesome Power of a Specific Transformation

Of the five structure examples, Phrases appeared the most succinct and easiest to remember, so I chose to use this method. Another may work better for you.

Step 3
PROOF

A Little Goes a Long Way

Proof can come in the form of illustrations, statistics, cited research, examples, and a mass of other ways.

Don't give in to the dark side of speaking. It beckons you to add illustration after illustration, story after story, statistic after statistic, until, finally, you have wandered so far away from the original point that no one knows where you are, or how you will return.

Just as your POINTS should point directly to the PURPOSE, your PROOF should be aimed precisely at your POINTS.

So far we have:

PURPOSE
⬆
POINTS
⬆
PROOF

Everything points back to the purpose of the engagement.

In a few minutes you'll get twenty-five places for good proof. Go after your sources with focus. Write down your points, and, as you find quotations, stories, etc., make sure they fit the purpose of the talk and relate specifically to the point.

Three Sweet Rules of PROOF

Rule 1 – Honestly Now

Be truthful. If the story is not yours, do not rearrange the names and tell the story as if it happened to you.

There's an old preacher's joke about the visiting preacher who stood at the door after the message to shake hands. A young man shook his hand and said, "Dullest talk I ever heard." Other nice members came through and shook his hand saying things like: "Wonderful." "Great job." Soon the same young man appeared again and said, "Horrible, just horrible!" Of course the preacher started getting nervous so he pulled a deacon to the side and inquired about the man. "Don't pay him any mind," said the deacon. "He's a little slow and cannot think for himself. He just goes around repeating what he's heard other people say."

First, that joke is old, so never use it. The audience will not think you are original or funny.

Second, we had a man speak to our church who told the story as if it happened to him. He never said he was kidding. And I know that it didn't happen to him. How do you think this made him look?

It's fine to use exaggeration to make a story funny as long as the audience understands what's happening, but don't lie.

Also, don't make up evidence to support your point. No tweaking the statistics. No editing the text and leaving out important words.

Rule 2 – Expose

Always reveal your sources.

- "Mark Twain wrote in . . ."
- "President Lincoln, when addressing the troops at . . ."
- "CNN reported last night . . ."
- "The *USA Today* newspaper printed the following chart in the Life section . . ."

You get the idea. You don't have to go into deep detail, just make it clear that you are not making it up and they can look it up if they want.

Rule 3 – Avoid Tired, Trite, and Overused Phrases

You want your words to be fresh and lively. *Avoid using lazy fillers* when providing proof. Stay away from phrases like

"That reminds me of a story I once heard . . ."

"Here's a funny thing that happened to me . . ."

"I love the illustration about . . ."

"A wise person once said . . . "

In fact, any "once" is off limits. Once said, once wrote, once thought, once considered, once . . .

Which of the following is stronger?

- "Mark Twain once wrote in one of his books . . ."
- "Mark Twain took a passionate stand on race relations in '*Huckleberry Finn.*"

Be specific and colorful in your wording.

Twenty-Five Places To Find Good Stuff

1. Life!

People magazine has a million readers a week and even more online. Do you think we like to hear about the lives of other people? You know it. I know what you're thinking. "But nobody would want to hear about my dull life." Wrong. First, I'll bet it's not as dull as you think. Second, as long as it's happening to you and not them, the audience will be thrilled to listen.

Your life is the best source of proof if

- It relates to the point.
- You can tell it well.
- You don't look like a hero. Self-effacing stories are the best.

Another reason your life is the best place for proof is its originality. No one has heard the story, and if they have they'll want to hear it again if it's good.

In fact, people will start to request certain stories from your life. For years I tried to avoid telling the same story if some people in the audience had heard me before. What a mistake. They would come up afterwards and say, "Why didn't you tell the story about . . . ? I told my friend it was great and how funny it was, and you didn't tell it." You'll even have people come up to you before a speech and say, "I heard you at (name of the venue), so could you please tell the story about the time you . . . "

How to know when you have a good life illustration:

- Emotional Extremes: If something happened to you where you wept, lost your temper, got embarrassed, did something stupid, or exhibited some other emotional outburst you hold the keys to a great illustration if you can tie it to a lesson learned that relates to the purpose of your talk.

- Surprise Encounters: Have you met someone famous or been confused for a celebrity? Did you fail to recognize someone you should have known, like a sister?

- Laughter: When you tell a friend something that happened to you and they laugh, mark it down. Maybe you can use it in a talk if it's appropriate.

- Keep Your Antenna Up: Most people flow through life with poor reception. Nothing "significant" happens to them because they are not tuned in. Keep your antenna up by asking, "What has happened today that someone could learn from?"

Keep a Journal or a Recorder or a Note Pad near You

You must write down what happens to you. You will not remember it. My friend Greg has had more bizarre things happen to him than anyone I know—of course he thinks they're normal until I fill him in on the truth. It's amazing the number of things that have happened to him that he forgets until something triggers the memory.

There's no need to go into great detail. Maybe you just need a few key words to bring it to mind. Maybe a brief outline would work.

A Lesson from the Pizza Place

Here's an example of what I've been telling you about. A friend and I went to get pizza at the Mellow Mushroom, and he wanted to learn about humor in speaking. Well, I can talk seriously about being funny for hours. We ordered and I went on and on, hardly taking a breath. We each emptied two sixteen-ounce glasses of Coke.

The waiter, Chris, approached the table and said, "Guys it's almost been an hour since your order. If you complain I'm sure the manager will give you your meal free." I wanted the free meal, but I sure didn't want to complain. It's just not my style in a restaurant, but I didn't need to. A few minutes later Chris returned giving us the thumbs up sign. "It's all taken care of, no worries."

Now I don't know much about being a waiter, but I do know that's the best way to get a great tip!

I can use that story to when I talk to groups about

- Customer service
- Friendliness
- Personality
- Initiative
- Ingenuity
- Rapport

Goal Story from My Life:

"In third grade my mom decided to sign me up for Pee Wee football. The name alone should have served as warning, but she proceeded. It was *her* goal for me to play. However, it was not *my* goal. Being a crafty elementary student at the time, I stuffed all my gear in a trash bag and put it behind the hot water heater. Having "misplaced" the equipment, I ended my football career abruptly, much to the disappointment of my mom.

I use this story to illustrate that forcing a goal on another just doesn't work. Your life is a rich source of information and inspiration.

2. Quotations

Use quotations to provide support because:

- Quoting a competent authority shows the depth of your research.

- It proves that your idea has broad appeal and acceptance.

- It is an easy way to add richness to your talk.

Online resources include the Quotations Page and Quoteland.com. Brainy Quote organizes quotations alphabetically by author or subject and Bartleby.com tends to be more literary in nature.

Or you can go to your favorite search engine and enter "quotations goals."

The library is a great source for books of quotations. Again, make sure you ask the librarian to guide you if you need help locating anything. And while you're at the library, don't overlook biographies as sources of great quotations. This is an excellent way to find a lesser-known quotation by a person whom you admire.

Goal Quote:

> "Fact: You will never realize more than a small fraction of your potential as a wandering generality. You must become a meaningful specific." —Zig Ziglar, *Over the Top*

3. News

Rely on television to stay current with national and international affairs. You get a good overview of what is happening. If anything is reported that ties into your message, use it. However, do be aware of the fact that a news organization may have a certain slant to its reporting. The best way to get a balanced view of a topic is to watch several different news programs that espouse several different philosophies and viewpoints.

Using stories from the news will show that you're current, knowledgeable, and able to relate your topic to contemporary events.

You can currently access many news services online. Some popular sites include CNN.com; ABC news; Fox News, which has a more conservative slant; CBS News; MSNBC, which has a more liberal slant; and the BBC, which is more international in its reporting.

Goal News:

> The *NBC Nightly News* reported last Monday on a study that revealed a trend among college students that might be of interest to you as you consider establishing clear goals for your life. Among first-year college students, 1 percent definitely know their life direction, 5 percent have a strong feeling, and a full 94 percent are undecided.

4. Newspapers

When traveling and you want to use some local flavor, tap into the local newspaper. You can mention an article, a person, an event, anything to show you are interested in the people who live in the area where you are speaking and their lives.

Before going to a city, log on to the Internet and do a city search of your destination. Print or write down anything interesting that you feel you can use to connect with your audience. Great online resources include Online Newspapers.com, which compiles thousands of newspapers and is organized geographically; *USA Today*, which is a good general United States source; and the *New York Times*, which covers national and international news as well as news specific to New York.

If you pick up a paper at the newsstand, go ahead and cut out the article you will use as proof.

The audience doesn't mind you reading during your presentation if you are holding the source of the information.

Goal Newspaper Story:

> A *USA Today* article in May of last year reported on a study of setting goals and the effects it has on overall achievement. I've highlighted a few of the excerpts. Listen to these interesting thoughts.

5. Movies

Do you want to know how to go to the movies for free all year long? No, don't sneak in the side door! Use the movies in your talks. If you are able to weave the meaning of a movie into your talk *and* you are getting paid to speak, it's like going to the movies free.

Don't you think mentioning the movie in a way that captivates your audience is worth the money that you paid to see it? You bet!

The best way to watch a movie for benefit is to go with your topic in mind. You don't have to concentrate on your presentation, just be aware of where you're headed. When a scene jumps out at you, mentally log it and write it down later.

One of the industries I speak to regularly is life insurance producers. My first wife passed away at age 27. Our son was only 5 weeks old. One afternoon I watched *Groundhog Day*, and a stereotypical insurance salesman approached Bill Murray's character. The scene painfully demonstrates why 98 percent of society runs from insurance salesmen. That clip works great when speaking to those groups. We get to laugh at the stereotype and discover how to eliminate it.

One word of caution: if you are planning to use a movie clip in a live setting, you must purchase a license that gives you permission to show it. (That's what the illegible FBI warning is about at the beginning of every movie you rent.) It would be a sad thing if you speak on ethics and get arrested the next day for illegally showing a video during your presentation! You can get all the details from the Motion Picture Licensing Corporation (www.mplc.com), or call 1-800-462-8855.

For ideas of movies to use in your talks, you can turn to online reviews. Some good sources are the Internet Movie Database, Rotten Tomatoes, and Entertainment Weekly.

Goal Movie Illustration:

> In *Remember the Titans*, Denzel Washington plays a football coach who must win every game in order to keep his position. One loss and he loses it all. (Play movie clip when he realizes the stakes of each game.) That type of focus will fuel you. The goal was so specific and so tied to a time frame that it couldn't be mistaken.

6. Songs

Music, as you know, has charms that soothe the savage breast (William Congreve, *The Mourning Bride*). Rarely do audiences become savage, but music is definitely a good way to tap into an emotion, a lesson, or an experience. People tend to respond to music different than they do other types of media, and it's an effective way to invite your audience to look at your points in a new way.

A few rules for using songs:

- It's better to quote the lyrics than play the song.

- If you play the song the sound system must be perfect and every word clearly understandable.

- If you sing you: (A) must be able to sing and (B) should choose to sing *a cappella* (without music) than with music, because it's so unusual.

- Sing or play what is critical to your point, nothing more.

- You must have a CCLI license to use music in a public forum. Get it here: http://www.ccli.com

Online resources for music and lyrics include Real Lyrics. com, Lyrics.com, Lyrics Search Engine (lyrics.astraweb.com), and Lyrics World.

Goal Song:

"Time in a Bottle" by Jim Croce

Play a portion of the song, or read the lyrics you want to emphasize.

"But there never seems to be enough time
To do the things you want to do
Once you find them"

When you work toward a goal, you do save time. It's like saving time in a bottle, because you eliminate, or at least minimize, wasted time.

7. Poetry

If you decide to use poetry it must be good and clearly tie to the point. Although poetry is a powerful medium there are so many interpretations to one poem that you must choose one with an understood meaning.

Use poetry effectively by reading with meter. Each poem has its own voice and pace. An uninspired reading will not support your point; it will hurt it.

Online resources include A Poetry-Lover's Guide To the World-Wide Web, Pre-1950 and Post-1950, and Poets' Corner (theotherpages.org/poems).

Goal Poetry:

>This is a long poem, but it would be a solid point supporter or close to the concept of setting your personal goals and not just following others.

The Calf-Path
by Sam Walter Foss
(1858–1911)

I.

One day, through the primeval wood,
A calf walked home, as good calves should;

II.

But made a trail all bent askew,
A crooked trail as all calves do.
Since then three hundred years have fled,
And, I infer, the calf is dead.
But still he left behind his trail,
And thereby hangs my moral tale.
The trail was taken up next day,
By a lone dog that passed that way.
And then a wise bellwether sheep,
Pursued the trail o'er vale and steep;
And drew the flock behind him too,
As good bellwethers always do.

And from that day, o'er hill and glade.
Through those old woods a path was made.

III.

And many men wound in and out,
And dodged, and turned, and bent about;
And uttered words of righteous wrath,
Because 'twas such a crooked path.
But still they followed—do not laugh—
The first migrations of that calf.
And through this winding wood-way stalked,
Because he wobbled when he walked.

IV.

This forest path became a lane,
that bent, and turned, and turned again.
This crooked lane became a road,
Where many a poor horse with his load,
Toiled on beneath the burning sun,
And traveled some three miles in one.
And thus a century and a half,
They trod the footsteps of that calf.

V.

The years passed on in swiftness fleet,
The road became a village street;
And this, before men were aware,
A city's crowded thoroughfare;
And soon the central street was this,
Of a renowned metropolis;
And men two centuries and a half,
Trod in the footsteps of that calf.

VI.

Each day a hundred thousand rout,
Followed the zigzag calf about;
And o'er his crooked journey went,

The traffic of a continent.
A Hundred thousand men were led,
By one calf near three centuries dead.
They followed still his crooked way,
And lost one hundred years a day;
For thus such reverence is lent,
To well-established precedent.

VII.

A moral lesson this might teach,
Were I ordained and called to preach;
For men are prone to go it blind,
Along the calf-paths of the mind;
And work away from sun to sun,
To do what other men have done.
They follow in the beaten track,
And out and in, and forth and back,
And still their devious course pursue,
To keep the path that others do.
They keep the path a sacred groove,
Along which all their lives they move.
But how the wise old wood gods laugh,
Who saw the first primeval calf!
Ah! many things this tale might teach—
But I am not ordained to preach.

Too many willingly follow the calf path. It's well worn for that reason, but that doesn't make it the best path for you. Make a new path that others may follow if they wish. But you take the first step.

8. Books

The best advice I can give you for life and for speaking is to read. Reading creates breadth and depth simultaneously. Reading spurs your creativity and helps you think critically.

Build a library of various styles. Of course, as you are doing right know, build a library of communication resources.

There are many ways to keep up with the information and examples you get from reading. I like to underline a good story, or quotation, and then place the page number on the inside cover of the book with a description: "17, paragraph relating to leadership."

Before going to a bookstore, do some online research if you can. Write down the books you want, and then call the store to make sure they have them.

Some useful online sites that you can use are Amazon and Barnes & Noble's online site (www.bn.com). Both offer used and out-of-print book services, along with reviews, summaries and other recommendations. And if you have a local Barnes & Noble store, you can actually search your local store's stock online and reserve a copy of the book. The booksellers at the store will pull your book and set it aside for you to pick up the next time you go in. For a wide variety of Christian books, Christianbook.com offers books, eBooks, music, DVDs, and more.

Goal Book Excerpt:

> John Renesch writes in *Goal Setting*, "It has been my experience that a major source of dissatisfaction experienced by many people is that they are not achieving the goals that they really want!"
>
> These people, even though they are fantastic achievers and very effective individuals, were striving for goals they felt they "should" have—things they were impressed with as being what they should work for in their lives.
>
> Sound crazy? You bet it is. However, many people are very busy striving for goals they've set without really personally *owning* them or taking personal responsibility for them."

That's why it's critical to get specific. That's why you and I must create goals of focus. Here's how.

9. Conversations

There are no casual conversations. You never know when a small bit of wisdom can show itself.

You can get the most from your conversations by doing this:

- Learn to listen. Concentrate and focus on the individual. Give him or her your full attention. If you're with a group someone might throw out a great line that you want to remember.

- Ask, "Can I quote you?" Let the person know that you found what he said interesting. Ask him to repeat it so you can be sure to get it right.

- Write it down. Keep paper scraps, 3 x 5 cards, or whatever you want, in your pockets. That way you can write it down immediately. Plus the person you are speaking with will feel important since you took time to write it down right away.

Goal Conversation:

Recently I was talking to a friend of mine about his workout schedule. I asked, "What are you trying to accomplish?"

"Well, I'd really like to lose some weight by summer."

That's not very specific, so I went deeper, "How much?"

"I guess about fifteen or twenty pounds. You know, enough to not get embarrassed at the beach."

Do you notice anything wrong with his goal?

"Some weight . . . by summer . . . I guess." None of those are specific enough. The first key we need to consider is The Awesome Power of A Specific Date.

10. Benches

Take a seat at the park or the mall and watch people. Here are some things to look for:

- Facial expressions. How many people walk through the mall looking happy?

- Speed. Do most appear in a hurry, or are they taking their time?

- Volume. Do you see any parents arguing with their children? Any person being obviously loud just to get attention? Any shoplifters being chased by security?

- Packages. Anyone over burdened by bags?

Take the time to watch. This may not give you anything scientific to cite, but it will increase your power of observation about general human behavior.

Goal Bench Observation:

> Last Saturday, I planted myself on a bench near a mall entrance. One lady entered with a determined look and a fast pace. Another walked in and appeared to have no particular purpose, allowing herself to be distracted by displays and the activity of the mall.
>
> The first probably needed to get a specific item, by a specific time. The second seemed to lack focus.
>
> Less than five minutes later the first individual rushed toward the exit with bag in hand. Goal accomplished! The second may still be wandering. Who knows?

Setting a specific goal and crafting a plan to reach that goal will help you avoid a lot of wasted time. Specificity of purpose is key to your success.

11. Bumper Stickers

These are fine as soft fillers for light laughs, but don't expect the audience to fall over. Plus it still needs to tie in to your point and purpose.

One sticker reads: "Since I gave up hope, I feel much better." You might use that line in a talk about how seriously we take our lives.

Be cautious about using bumper stickers for humor. First, know what is being implied. The audience may take it one way when you mean something else. Second, many stickers are filthy and not appropriate.

You can sit by a traffic light and look at bumper as cars pass or you can go to Stickerzone.com or Instant Attitudes (www.instantattitudes.com/lists.html).

Goal Bumper Sticker:

Maybe you've seen this bumper sticker:

Nothing is impossible..
for the person
who doesn't have to do it!
©WWW.STICKERZONE.COM

When we have no true direction, we have no true expectation. The third key we need to look at is The Awesome Power of a Specific Plan.

12. Magazines

One magazine you must subscribe to as a speaker: *Reader's Digest*. President Reagan (known as the Great Communicator) pointed to *Reader's* as his number one source of illustrations. And it is available online as well as in print.

Other magazines that will provide a lot of material for proof are *Newsweek, US News and World Report,* and *People.* You can scan the magazine rack of your local bookstore and find a publication on just about every subject imaginable: business, entrepreneurship, gardening, computers, cooking . . . you get the picture. For articles relating to general topics of interest to most people, good selections are the *New Yorker, The Economist, Forbes, Atlantic Monthly,* and *Vanity Fair,* to name a few.

Goal Magazine Article:

From *Reader's Digest*

From "Discover Your Achievement Zone" by Edwin Kiester, Jr. and Sally Valente Kiester

"The ability to devote unswerving attention to a task can produce success in any field. On the other hand, being unable to stay in a zone can turn a sure winner into an also-ran. At the 1992 U.S. Olympic trials, decathlon star Dan O'Brien began by setting such a record pace in the contest's events that a place on the team seemed certain. That's when he relaxed and stumbled in the pole vault — failing to clear a height that he had reached hundreds of times before. Unable, as he admitted later, to "get his head together," he tried and failed twice more. Despite O'Brien's physical abilities, a mental lapse had dashed his Olympic hopes.

"Most of us can sympathize with O'Brien. You've probably had those frustrating times when you couldn't seem to get your brain going. You've sat blankly in front of the computer screen, struggling to find the right words.

You've stared at the budget figures, unable to get your mind around them. And yet you've also known states of high concentration—when you've gotten your best work done at a fast pace. How can you get yourself into your most productive state, your own personal zone?"

The next few minutes I would talk about the power of concentration and visualization as it relates to The Awesome Power of a Specific Focus.

13. Ezines

What could be better than getting great illustrations and ideas right in your e-mail?

Here are some places to get free ezines: FreeEzineWeb.com, New-List (ezine-universe.com),and EzineLocator.

Locate an ezine related to your topic and subscribe. Most will give you access to back issues and you will find more than enough articles, quotations, and other resources to pull from.

Goal Ezine Excerpt:

> Just a couple of minutes ago I went to ezinelocater.com and signed up for a personal achievement newsletter that sends a daily achievement quote. Immediately I got the following e-mail:
>
>> Reviewing your goals daily is a crucial part of your success and must become part of your routine. Each morning when you wake up read your list of goals that are written in the positive. Visualize the completed goal, see the new home; smell the leather seats in your new car; feel the cold, hard cash in your hands. Then each night, right before you go to bed, repeat the process. This process will start both your subconscious and conscious mind on working towards the goal. This will also begin to

replace any of the negative self-talk you may have and replace it with positive self-talk.

I can't promise that you'll get as timely an e-mail as the above, but it fits perfectly with the message we're building.

14. Analogies

An analogy helps you clarify what you are presenting by connecting it with another concept so a visual picture is formed. Most of the time the word pictures you use are not similar, but in using an analogy you can draw a point of comparison between two seemingly very different things.

Create your own analogies by using "like" as your comparison tool. For example:

"Going through your day mentally first thing in the morning is like traveling into the future and returning. You actually get to see where you are going before it happens."

Goal Analogy:

"Setting a goal without a date of completion is like setting sail without a destination."

15. Interviews

This is the most overlooked way to add strength to your points. It's overlooked because it's not as easy as opening a book or going to a Website.

1. Make a list of names that are either recognized or can speak directly about the message you are presenting. The higher the recognition the more difficult it will be to make contact. But don't give up; many well-known people are accessible and often happy to share their experiences and insights.

2. If possible, make it a person that people will be slightly awed that you approached and questioned.

3. Have your questions prepared ahead of time and use a maximum of five. If you know the person well, you can use more, but be sure to respect the friendship and not take advantage of a busy person's generosity with his or her time.

4. If it is a well-known person, you will likely speak first to an assistant or public relations person. Have a good idea of your availability and try to be flexible. You'll have a better chance of landing an interview. Be clear how much time you'll need. You may be asked to submit questions in advance, so be prepared for that.

5. Be punctual with your phone call or appointment. If you do plan to record the interview, be sure to ask permission first. Ask your questions and any follow up questions, carefully recording the answers. After the answers thank the person for the time and end the conversation. Be sure that you don't take more time than you requested. Not being obnoxious and trying to talk for hours may endear you to him or her and keep the door open for future interviews.

6. Have a tape recorder or a notebook. Write fast. Do not ask for a repeat while you write everything down. Get it the first time.

7. Send a handwritten thank-you note to the person you interview.

Goal Interview:

Interview with John McLinburg, Ph.D.

Paul: I will be speaking on The Awesome Power of Goal Achieving. What is the most important aspect in goal setting in your opinion?

Step 3: PROOF

John: Getting a precise picture of your intended outcome. You must do more than just write it down in positive terms. You must make your brain believe it has already occurred. I call this "making the future the present."

Paul: Making the future the present? What does that mean?

John: Ok, the future in the present means you so believe in your goal that it is real to you. Not real in the future. Real in the present. The mind then takes the circumstances of your life and attempts to shape all of them to the goal. Since it believes the goal has already taken place it must do whatever is necessary to keep the belief in place.

Paul: Can you give me an example?

John: OK, let's keep it simple. Let's say that you want to lose twenty pounds. Picture yourself twenty pounds lighter. Imagine how you feel. Set your scale back. Put up a picture of "you" twenty pounds less. Convince your mind that you *are* that weight. It will now take steps to keep you there. Your desire for desserts will decrease. You will feel an urge to exercise or watch the next meal closer when you blow it.

But it's not just weight. If you imagine you're rich, your conversations will change. Your mind will help you open doors to the next level. Your consciousness will be altered toward money.

That's a short part of the interview, but you can see how helpful this avenue would be.

16. Statistics

Scientific proof is hard to beat. Be sure that any statistics you use are true and not slanted. Make sure you cite the source. Tom Peters rocked the business world when he revealed that *In Search of Excellence* used biased stats to create a business model that the authors desired. You want to avoid this type of notoriety.

Online statistic sources include the U.S. Census Bureau for demographic information and analyses and Statistics.com, a searchable database of statistical information and data sources on the Internet.

Goal Statistic:

> In 1953 researchers polled the graduating class of Yale University and found that 3 percent of the graduates practiced goal setting and had a set of clearly defined written goals.
>
> In 1973 researchers went back and visited the class of '53 and found that the 3 percent of the graduates who had the clear and written goals had amassed a fortune worth more than the other 97 percent combined. This is powerful evidence that goal setting is a proven process in creating and defining success.
>
> What does that mean in this day and age? Decades later, will we reflect on the strides of our lives and feel satisfied? Setting specific goals can lead to incredible results.

17. Stories

What separates stories from other forms of illustrations is they are usually longer—five minutes or more—and they engage multiple emotions such as humor, sadness, anger, compassion. They can be about family, friends, even strangers; it doesn't matter. Books and magazines contain incredible stories for you to use. *Reader's Digest* comes to mind because each month it is filled with human-interest stories.

Quick Story Telling Tips:

- Know your story inside out; don't fumble.
- Make the tie into the message apparent.

- Don't let it embarrass anyone—unless the story is about you or you have permission.

- Don't let it overshadow your speech. It's possible to have a story so good that people remember it, but not your point.

The Website Storytelling Power will give you all the articles and ideas you need to become a powerful storyteller.

Goal Story:

> Retell the story from Zig Ziglar's book *Over the Top*, pages 167–169. He tells the story of Tom Hartman whose weight loss moved him from 350 pounds to 225 pounds at a height of 6'4". I can use this story to drive home my last point The Awesome Power of Specific Transformation.

18. Definitions

Use definitions sparingly. They can make you sound like every other speaker who uses the same idea.

How many times have you heard a presenter say, "Webster defines . . ."

A better way to use definitions is: "A goal is defined as the purpose toward which an endeavor is directed; an objective. That's nice and formal, but what does it really mean? It's one thing to define the word goal; it's another to set defining goals."

Dictionary.com will keep you from pulling out a heavy hardback dictionary. It compiles definitions from numerous reputable dictionaries such as Webster's. Random House and American Heritage. While you're there click on the tab for Thesaurus.com. It's a great resource for more specific, colorful, and interesting synonyms.

Wordorigins.com shares, among other information, the origins words and phrases, which can be interesting and informative.

Check out Daffynitions for a few free funny definitions. Example: Progress: What you get when each mistake is a new one. It's a creative way to inject humor into your talk.

Goal Definition:

> Motivational speaker Earl Nightingale defined goals in this way, "Success is the progressive realization of a worthy ideal." Success is the accomplishment of a goal. You reach success through a progressive realization. It doesn't happen all at once; it takes a plan. His second point, a worthy ideal, gives us a guide for measuring whether or not it is worth our while to pursue a goal. It must be more than a good idea—a good ideal. Let's take it a step further.

19. Examples

Examples put your points in action.

The next time you are in the audience listen for the number of times the speaker says, "For example." He's pointing out that he will be linking what he just stated to show it in action.

If he's talking about gravity, he'll grab an object and say, "For example, when I let go of this pencil it will fall down, not up." I know, I know, it's a stupid example, but you get it.

You can do the same for any concept you're presenting. I usually ask myself, "How can I make this real?"

When speaking about time management I thought about the idea of relativity. But that can be tough for people to grasp. So I asked, "How many of you think a year is a long time?" Several hands went up. I asked more questions until finally, "How many of you think ten seconds is a long time?" No one raised a hand.

I called for a volunteer from the audience, asked her to pull up her sleeve, struck a match, and said, "I am going to put this flame against your forearm for ten seconds. Do you think ten seconds will seem long?" She agreed that it would. I went on to talk about time being relative to our circumstances.

Those types of examples are everywhere, or you can create them yourself.

Goal Example:

"Raise your hand if you saved money toward a purchase in the last year. OK, sir, what did you save toward? A vacation, excellent. Where did you go? Hawaii! Excellent again! How long did it take you to save? Eighteen months. Was it worth it?"

That's a simple example of using the audience. Real dialogue takes place. Interaction takes place. And I can go on to talk about the reward of setting and achieving the goal. I can also talk about the how specific the goal was in terms of time, money and location.

20. Syndicated Columns

It's astonishing the type of advice people will write to a columnist about. Ann Landers and others, including talk shows, are a rich source of personal experiences from across the globe. Most of the time you can use these as examples of how not to behave, or what not to do.

The Washington Post's Ann Landers Column and Dear Abby are interesting resources for finding real-life stories and situations that might illustrate your points. Search the Internet for syndicated columns by local writers. They are a gold mine of human-interest stories.

Don't be afraid to e-mail the writer. You just might get a reply, and you will be able to use that to your advantage during your speech. It's always more powerful to speak from a personal encounter.

Goal Advice Column:

Jeffrey H. Gitmer has a syndicated column called *Sales-Moves*. Here's a courtesy excerpt from a goal column. Visit: www.Gitomer.com to read more.

How can a pad of Post-it notes put you on the path to greater achievement?

Follow the formula…

1. **Write down big ones** On 3x3 yellow Post-it notes, write down your three prime goals in short phrases with bold letters (get $25,000 funding for business; buy a new car; land a new client).

2. **Write down small ones** Write down your three secondary goals in short phrases with bold letters (read book by Dale Carnegie; organize desk; build new closet).

3. **Post them on your bathroom mirror where you can see them twice a day** You are forced to look at them every morning and evening.

4. **Keep looking and reading until you act** You will look at them twice every day. You will read them aloud twice a day. You will look at them and read them until you are sick of looking at them, and reading them—and then you will begin to accomplish them. By posting the goal in the bathroom you are consciously reminded of your goals several times a day. From there your subconscious gets into the act. Gnawing away at your inner soul until you are driven to take positive action. Achievement actions. At last you can say the magic words … scream them—I did it! (Screaming positive things always feels wonderful.)

5. **Start your day by looking at your successes** After your goal is achieved take it off the bathroom

mirror and triumphantly post it on your bedroom mirror so you can see your success every time you look in that mirror. Not only does it feel great, but you also get to set the tone for a successful day every day first thing in the morning. It also gets you motivated to keep achieving more.

The program is simple. The program works. The results will change your attitude.

The results will change your outlook about your capability of success achievement.

The results will change your life.

I urge you to give this process a solid thirty-day trial. Use more small goals than big goals at first, so you can get immediate gratification. Post it. Post haste.

I hope you realize the full achievement of your goals.

21. Television

The news, sitcoms, dramas, you name it and they contain rich sources of material for your messages. Plus it's so easy to use.

"The other day when I was watching (name of the show), (name of character) said . . . Here's what that means to us."

"On (name of show) last week (talk about the plot). That same pattern occurs in our lives. First, I want to explain why that happens. Then what we can do about it."

Used correctly television can become a valuable rapport tool. It connects you to the audience because you are sharing a common cultural experience. You are taking something that your audience may have only considered to be entertainment and you are giving it relevance for their lives. You may very well change the way your listeners observe the world.

It keeps you current. Since new programs come out all the time you don't have to focus on episode #183 of *The Andy Griffith Show* (but you can since it never seems to get old!).

Goal Television Show:

> Since I just mentioned *The Andy Griffith Show*, I might as well use it now.
>
> "In episode #43 of *The Andy Griffith Show*—and if any of you can immediately name the title of the show we need to get you into *serious* therapy—Aunt Bea makes her famous kerosene pickles.
>
> "Andy hates them. Barney hates them. No one can tolerate them. But Andy wants to save Aunt Bea's feelings so he switches the bad pickles for a nice store brand.
>
> "The problem starts when they brag about how good the pickles are to Aunt Bea. So what does she do? She wants to enter them in the county fair pickle contest. What are Andy and Barney to do? How will Andy protect Aunt Bee, keep the contest fair, and come off glistening in the end as the wise sheriff?
>
> "Well, that's not important. Here's what is. If Andy had planned ahead he could have foreseen the outcome. Sure, the story wouldn't have been as good, or as funny, but it would have saved good-boy Andy a heap o' headaches.
>
> "The same is true for us when we plan ahead. We can avoid embarrassment, misunderstandings, and mistakes by putting a plan behind our goals. Here's how."

22. Jokes

Most jokes are "corny." They get sympathy laughs, but not real ones if you're not careful. Before using a joke try it out on several of your friends just to be safe. If eight out of ten laugh immediately, then use it if it applies to the message.

Online sources for jokes to use in your talk include Official Home of Fun with greetings, games, and clean jokes; Scatty.com, with more than 3,500 clean fun family jokes in lots of categories for everyone to enjoy; Good Clean Fun—no obscene language or vulgarity here—however, "religion" and "politics" are always fair game; Barking Spider, with all clean jokes, all the time; Kids' Jokes, with more than 2,000 clean kids jokes for children of any age and lots of categories (animal jokes, knock knock jokes, and silly jokes); and JokesEveryDay.Com, a daily clean joke list.

Goal Joke:(It's a long one)

> So we were lying on our backs on the grass in the park next to our hamburger wrappers, my 14-year-old son and I, watching the clouds loiter overhead, when he asked me, "Dad, why are we here?"
>
> And this is what I said:
>
> "I've thought a lot about it, son, and I don't think it's all that complicated. I think maybe we're here just to teach a kid how to bunt or eat sunflower seeds without using his hands.
>
> "We're here to pound the steering wheel and scream as we listen to the game on the radio, twenty minutes after we pulled into the garage. We're here to look all over, give up and then find the ball in the hole.
>
> "We're here to watch, at least once, as the pocket collapses around John Elway, and it's fourth-and-never. Or as the count goes to 3 and 1 on Mark McGwire with bases loaded, and the pitcher begins wishing he'd gone

on to medical school. Or as a little hole you couldn't get a skateboard through suddenly opens in front of Jeff Gordon with a lap to go.

"We're here to wear our favorite sweat-soaked Boston Red Sox cap, torn Slippery Rock sweatshirt and the Converses we lettered in, on a Saturday morning with nowhere we have to go and no one special we have to be.

"We're here to photograph a six-point elk and finally get the f-stop right, or to tie the perfect fly, make the perfect cast, catch absolutely nothing and still call it a perfect morning.

"We're here to nail a yield sign with an apple core from half a block away. We're here to make our dog bite on the same lame fake throw for the gazillionth time. We're here to win the stuffed bear or go broke trying.

"I don't think the meaning of life is gnashing our bicuspids over what comes after death but tasting all the tiny moments that come before it. We're here to be the coach when Wendell, the one whose glasses always fog up, finally makes the only perfect backdoor pass all season. We're here to be there when our kid has three goals and an assist. And especially when he doesn't.

"We're here to be able to do a one-and-a-half for our grandkids. Or to stand at the top of our favorite double black on a double-blue morning and overhear those five wonderful words: 'Highway's closed. Too much snow.'

"We're here to get the Frisbee to do things that would have caused medieval clergymen to burn us at the stake.

"I don't think we're here to make SportsCenter. The really good stuff never does. Like leaving Wrigley at 4:15 on a perfect summer afternoon and walking straight into Murphy's with half of section 503. Or finding ourselves with a free afternoon, a little red 327 fuel-injected 1962

Corvette convertible and an unopened map of Vermont's back roads.

"We're here to get the triple-Dagwood sandwich made and the football kicked off at the very second your sister begins tying up the phone until Tuesday.

"None of us are going to find ourselves on our deathbeds saying, 'Dang, I wish I'd spent more time on the Hibbings account.' We're going to say, 'That scar? I got that scar stealing a home run from Consolidated Plumbers!'

"See, grown-ups spend so much time doggedly slaving toward the better car, the perfect house, the big day that will finally make them happy when happy just walked by wearing a bicycle helmet two sizes too big for him. We're not here to find a way to heaven. The way is heaven. Does that answer your question, son?"

And he said, "Not really, Dad."

And I said, "No?"

And he said, "No, what I meant is, why are we here when Mom said to pick her up forty minutes ago?"

"When it comes to our goals it's not enough to ask questions, we need to understand those questions. It's not enough to make plans. We must understand why we make those plans. Filling up a page with good intentions won't cut it."

23. Success Stories

Use real people, their real names, and accurate accounts. The reason we love to hear about another's success is because it gives us hope. Maybe we can do the same thing. Maybe our story could possess the same ending.

Goal Success Story (from Bible Gateway)
http://www.gospelcom.net/actsi/solutions/failure1.htm

> It is well known that for twenty-eight years Abraham Lincoln experienced one failure after another. In 1833 he had a nervous breakdown. When he ran for speaker in 1838 he was defeated. In 1848 he lost re-nomination to Congress and was rejected for land officer in 1849. These failures didn't stop him from battling on. In 1854 he was defeated for the Senate. Two years later he lost the nomination for vice president and was again defeated for the Senate in 1858. Yet, despite it all, in 1860 he was elected president and went down in history as one of America's greatest presidents.
>
> Obviously, success isn't the absence of failure. It is having the determination to never quit, even in the face of stiff opposition. Almost every person who has achieved anything worthwhile with his or her life has not only experienced failure but has probably experienced it many times. Lincoln experienced several failures, but he was never a failure because he never gave up.
>
> Walt Disney was the same. He went broke several times and had a nervous breakdown before he became successful.
>
> Enrico Caruso failed so many times with his high notes that his voice teacher advised him to give up. He didn't. Instead, he persevered and became one of the world's greatest tenors.
>
> Albert Einstein and Werner von Braun both failed courses in math. Henry Ford was broke when he was 40. Thomas Edison's teacher called him a dunce, and later he failed more than 6,000 times before he perfected the first electric light bulb.
>
> Rather than having no goal, as Theodore Roosevelt wisely said, "Far better is it to dare mighty things, to win

glorious triumphs, even though checked by failure, than to take rank with those poor spirits who neither enjoy much nor suffer much, because they live in the gray twilight that knows neither victory nor defeat."

24. The Bible

Unless you primarily speak to Christian groups limit your use of this sacred text. Why do I say that? Because many people find it offensive. They feel that you are preaching and not presenting. No matter how good your intentions, you will shut people out of your message with too much scripture.

Recently I listened to a talk where the speaker started quoting a biblical passage early in his message. He made it obvious that unless the audience embraced the passage as Christians they could not "get" his speech.

You could tell that it made the crowd uncomfortable. And you could tell that he wouldn't have much of an impact that day.

If you would like personal advice on how to use scripture best in a message, I will say as someone who has been a minister for fifteen years that it's better to say too little and raise questions, than to say too much and close every mind in the room.

Here are some general tips:

- Quote the Bible as you would any other source.
- Use a modern translation.
- Know your audience. If they have a religious base you can use more.
- Watch the room. If the passage makes the group uneasy consider ways of clarifying the passage without causing offense.

Goal Bible Passage:

Luke 14: 25–32

> Large crowds were traveling with Jesus, and turning to them he said:
>
>> "If anyone comes to me and does not hate his father and mother, his wife and children, his brothers and sisters—yes, even his own life—he cannot be my disciple. And anyone who does not carry his cross and follow me cannot be my disciple.
>>
>> "Suppose one of you wants to build a tower. Will he not first sit down and estimate the cost to see if he has enough money to complete it. For if he lays the foundation and is not able to finish it, everyone who sees it will ridicule him, saying, 'This fellow began to build and was not able to finish.'
>>
>> "Or suppose a king is about to go to war against another king. Will he not first sit down and consider whether he is able with ten thousand men to oppose the one coming against him with twenty thousand? If he is not able, he will send a delegation while the other is still a long way off and will ask for terms of peace."
>
> "The awesome power of a specific plan can be fully realized when the cost is counted. Luke makes it clear. A lack of planning causes embarrassment and defeat. Here's how we can avoid both of those."

25. EVERYWHERE!

There is no limit to the amount of material you can find to support and describe your points. Literally, it's everywhere. Stay attuned. Write it down. Record it if you want. Just don't think for a moment that there is not a vast amount of ways you can bring your points to life.

When you hear other speakers tell great stories, or have great illustrations, don't think, "That stuff never happens to me," or "Why can't I find good material like that."

You have experiences ALL THE TIME that will prove valuable to the audience. You are valuable. And I've just given you plenty of links to find all the ways to prove your points that you will need.

Illustrative Connectedness

Your illustrations must always connect to each other, to the point, and to the purpose. You never want to use anything that makes the audience think, "What was that about?"

For every point locate ten illustrations. Print them out, write them down, whatever you want. From those ten use only the best two or three. Those will be the ones that meet the following criteria:

- Support your point

- Make the point come to life

- Tie the point to today so it's relevant

- Clarify the point

- Help the audience apply the point

- Create an "aha" moment where the people suddenly get what you're saying

- Do not overshadow the point

- Are not too difficult to understand, nor so simple that they are foolish

Irrefutable Law of Speaking
Between Illustrations Always Return to the Point.

If you link illustrations to each other without mentioning the point again, the audience will associate the present example with the previous one, not to the point.

You want interaction like this…

point > < illustration > < point > < illustration > point

Not like this…

point > < illustration > illustration > illustration

If you stack illustrations, you get further and further from the point. And the point gets more and more out of the mind of the audience.

That might seem minor, but it's not. I've got a friend that we joke on. His nickname is "Six Stories No Point." Listen to me; you don't want that title.

I know I've drilled this principle to the point of being obnoxious, but it's the key to success.

Elaborate

Illustrations will not take up the bulk of your speaking time; they are *starting places* for thoughts. After you tell a story or share a statistic you want to do several things for clarity:

8. Tie the illustration to the concept you are presenting. If 2 percent of people who are morning planners are the same 2 percent of those who achieve their goals, talk about its significance and **HOW** it relates to the point.

9. Bring life. You want the points to be alive. Expand the idea after the illustration and give it a pulse. The audience should be able to see the point in action in their lives. It answers, "**WHY** are you telling me this?"

10. Give steps. Showing people steps to alleviate their pain or problem tells how and why at the same time. Tell them **WHAT** to do.

If you were having a conversation with a friend and mentioned one of your points they would ask something like, "Well, what do you mean by that?" or "How can that help me?" or "Could you show me how I can use that?" or "Why is that true?"

Answer those same questions by elaborating on your points and proof.

Transitions

Transitions let the audience know you are moving between ideas or illustrations. If done well they're not noticeable. There is fluidity in a nice transition.

Here are several examples to get you started:

- In addition to what we just covered . . .
- Let's look at another point . . .
- Not only (repeat first point) there is also (state the second point) . . .
- Another area to consider . . .
- Here's what this means to us . . .

- Let's keep moving and discover another critical area . . .
- You can use that point alone, but there's more . . .
- Next . . .
- Let's look at this in a little larger context . . .
- Let me give you one more point to apply this week . . .
- Let's move onto step three in practice . . .

Step Three in Practice

Topic: Goal Achieving. **Title:** The Awesome Power of Goal Achieving

Purpose: Learn how to achieve goals, not just set them.

Points with Proof: (I would tie every illustration immediately back to the point)

- The Awesome Power of a Specific Desire
    1. What do you want more than anything? Be specific.
    2. How to write down everything you've ever wanted
    3. How to make it specific
    4. Why clarity is paramount—*USA Today* article
    5. 97 percent of people never set goals.
- The Awesome Power of a Specific Date
    1. Read section from *7 Habits*.

Step 3: PROOF

  2. Funny wedding story about setting "the date"
  3. How to determine what date to set

     Amount of planning

     Amount of effort

  4. Quote Zig Ziglar in *Over the Top*.
  5. The great calendar countdown technique

- The Awesome Power of a Specific Plan

  1. Joke about father and sun in park
  2. Story about my forgetting my glasses
  3. How to block distractions
  4. Jerusalem's walls in fifty-two days

     Workers, Guards, Opposition, Victory

- The Awesome Power of a Specific Focus

  5. Why vivid descriptions beat generic ones—psychology magazine page 82
  6. The power of autosuggestion by Napoleon Hill
  7. How to block distractions

     Breakthrough

     Build up

- The Awesome Power of a Specific Transformation

  1. Tie your goal to life.
  2. One-time success or lifetime triumph

95

3. How Walt Disney changed us forever
4. Pinpointing your specific transformation
    Need
    Desire
    Impact

Step 4
POWER

> *"It was not the object of Demosthenes to make the Athenians cry out 'What a splendid speaker!' but to make them say 'Let us march against Philip.'"*
>
> —John Stuart Mill,
> *On Education*, inaugural address on being installed as rector, University of St. Andrews (Scotland), February 1, 1867

Hey, just because you have some points and some proof, this does not mean you are ready for the circuit. There are several more areas that are CRITICAL to your message. These subtle areas are easy to forget when you're trying to get the meat of your message completed.

PURPOSE
↑
POINTS
↑
PROOF
↑
POWER

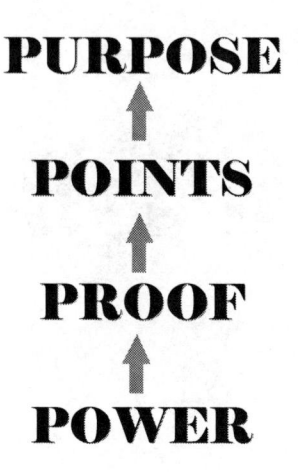

Don't forget: the POWER principles you are about to learn must ultimately point back to the original purpose of the talk.

Introducing

If someone is going to introduce you then make it good.

Irrefutable Law of Speaking
You Must Write Your Own Introduction.

First, leaving your intro to the fate of someone who will "make it up" puts you at a disadvantage. Who knows what will be said. The person might get the idea that it's a great time to try out some new comedy material and you're the joke.

Second, since everyone I've met is more than willing to read my introduction verbatim it's best not to run a risk. Plus, it's one more item the planner does not have to plan.

How to Write a Glowing Introduction

Fill in the following HONESTLY. Don't be arrogant, but don't be apprehensive, either.

1. List your education, current position, why you are credible, related experiences, books written, and family or friends. You can also list interesting things you have done that people would like to know about.

_____

_____

_____

_____

_____

2. Take the above information and write out a paragraph that explains who you are and why you are speaking to the group. This establishes credibility and creates anticipation for your talk.

_____

_____

_____

_____

_____

_____

_____

_____

3. Read your paragraph aloud and edit it for stuffiness or arrogance. It should read with ease, be light, and possibly even include some humor.

Here are introductions written by Patricia Fripp, a speaker and speaking coach. The first is her short version, then her longer versions. If you don't know about Patricia Fripp, visit her online (www.fripp.com).

Short:

> Patricia Fripp is an award-winning speaker and executive speech coach who delights audiences, electrifies executives who speak, and transforms sales teams. *Meetings and Conventions* magazine calls Patricia "one of the country's 10 most electrifying speakers." She is the author of two popular books, *Make It, So You Don't Have to Fake It!* and *Get What You Want.* Please make her welcome.

Intermediate:

> We are pleased to have with us today…
>
> Patricia Fripp, an award-winning speaker and speech coach who delights audiences, electrifies executives who speak, and transforms sales teams. *Meetings and Conventions* magazine calls Patricia "one of the country's 10 most electrifying speakers." She is author of *Make It! So You Don't Have to Fake It* and *Get What You Want,* and contributing author to *Speaking Secrets of the Masters* and *Insights Into Excellence.* Patricia was the first female president of the more than 4,000 member National Speakers Association and is a Hall of Fame recipient. Before becoming a speaker she enjoyed a highly successful career in a service industry. Please make her welcome.

Long Version:

"She is one of the most electrifying speakers in North America," says *Meetings and Conventions* magazine. Her clients agree. "Fripp is the most reliable, versatile, easy to work with, hassle-free, customer-friendly speaker we've ever booked," says Dan Maddux, executive director of the American Payroll Association.

Patricia Fripp was a successful entrepreneur in a service industry for twenty-four years. Today she is an award-winning international speaker who has addressed audiences on four continents.

The first woman president of the National Speakers Association (1984–85), she received their CSP (Certified Speaking Professional) designation in 1981 and their CPAE Hall of Fame Award in 1983 for professionalism and excellence in speaking. In 1996 she received the Cavett Award, the annual "Oscar" of the National Speakers Association. Fripp was the founder and president of the largest National Speakers Association chapter, NSA/Northern California. A leadership award, the "Frippy," has been named after her, and she is a member of the prestigious Speakers Roundtable, consisting of twenty-two of the most successful, in-demand speakers in the country.

Patricia Fripp's latest book is, *Make It, So You Don't Have to Fake It! 55 Fast-Acting Strategies for Long-Lasting Success*. Her book *Get What You Want*, has sold more than 40,000 copies. She is a contributing author to *Insights Into Excellence and Speaking Secrets of the Masters*, along with top national speakers Brian Tracy and Ken Blanchard. She is a regular columnist for national and international publications including *Western Association News*, and her online columns, "FrippNews" and "SpeakerFrippNews," have subscribers worldwide.

Patricia Fripp is the star of many training videos, including *Travel the Road to Success: An Adventure in Customer Service* and *Survival in the Workplace 2000*. A founding faculty expert of MentorU.com, an online mentoring and training company, and star of the Bullet Proof Manager series, sold in fifty-eight countries and translated into twenty-eight languages.

Fripp averages 130 programs yearly for corporations including IBM, Motorola, AT&T, and Sony, and for associations including the American Cemetery Association, the American Payroll Association, and the American Society of Association Executives. Her high-content, high-performance, user-friendly delivery brings uniform raves as she shares what she has learned from her wide experience with top corporations. Many of her clients use her in multiple slots on an ongoing basis, year after year. One of her favorite assignments is one-on-one speech coaching with executives and industry leaders on-site just before a conference or convention. She also coaches groups such as managers, salespeople, trainers, and marketers—people who need to direct, persuade, and sell their ideas. Fripp is known for transforming sales teams.

Her solid business background started when she went to work at age fifteen in her native England. At twenty, she arrived in San Francisco without a job, home, or contacts, just an invincible determination to succeed. By 1969 she was being featured in the media as one of the first women in the new field of men's hairstyling.

She was so successful that soon she was asked to give seminars for the hairstyling industry. Then her executive clients asked her to speak at their Rotary Clubs and sales meetings. She talked about customer service and business promotion, sharing funny and inspiring stories from "behind the chair." Gradually, she found that speaking had become her career.

The different lengths are obviously appropriate for different situations. You can discuss this with the person who books you and, if you have them ready, send multiple copies of your introduction for your introducer to choose from.

Tips on Introductions

First, always send your introduction ahead of time, so the introducer can look over it.

Second, always carry an extra copy with you in case it is forgotten or lost.

Third, don't underestimate the power of your introduction. I have. I scribbled out a soft introduction at an engagement and thought nothing about it. Later in the week a friend told me that he talked to someone at the meeting.

"You know what my friend was most impressed with?" He asked. "He was amazed that you were an author."

A good introduction would have mentioned a couple of the books and possibly sold some!

The Opening

Most speaking coaches will tell you that the way you start determines if you will win the audience or not. I'm not that sure. I do believe, however, that it determines how quickly you capture the audience.

Start slow and they *might* join you later. Start **bold** and they will hang on for the ride.

A solid opening is significant for four reasons:

- It creates rapport and likeability.
- It gets the audience in tune with your style.
- It loosens the audience and makes them comfortable.
- It allows you to prove that you are worth listening to.

The reason we didn't build the opening at the start of this book is because it's important to know where you are going before you get started. Once you have your points, only then can you determine how to get to them. Too many speakers begin with an opening *they* like, but one that has no relation to the subject.

Irrefutable Law of Speaking
An Opening Should Do Just That: Open the Hearts and Minds of the Listeners To Accept Your Message

Twelve Great Beginnings

I'll continue with the talk we're building, "The Awesome Power of Goal Achieving." Here are twelve ways the talk could start. They are *extremely abbreviated*, but it will give you the concept.

Step 4: POWER

1. Quote:

You can begin with a serious quote or a light one like the following:

> "Lily Tomlin says, 'The trouble with the rat race is that even if you win, you're still a rat.'
>
> "Do you ever feel that way? Do you ever feel like you just can't seem to get ahead? We'll I am about to share with you five concepts that will help you set and achieve goals, so you can escape the rat race."

2. Joke:

> "Listen to this comparison between work and prison.
>
> IN PRISON You spend the majority of your time in an 8x10 cell.
> AT WORK You spend most of your time in a 6x8 cubicle.
>
> IN PRISON You get three meals a day.
> AT WORK You get a break for one meal and you have to pay for it.
>
> IN PRISON You get time off for good behavior.
> AT WORK You get rewarded for good behavior with more work.
>
> IN PRISON A guard locks and unlocks all the doors for you.
> AT WORK You must carry around a security card and unlock and open all the doors yourself.
>
> IN PRISON You can watch TV and play games.
> AT WORK You get fired for watching TV and playing games.
>
> IN PRISON You get your own toilet.

AT WORK You have to share.

IN PRISON They allow your family and friends to visit.
AT WORK You cannot even speak to your family and friends.

IN PRISON There are wardens who are often sadistic.
AT WORK They are called supervisors.

IN PRISON You have unlimited time to read e-mail jokes.
AT WORK You get fired if you get caught.

NOW GET BACK TO WORK!

"Sometimes our lives feel like a prison. But the truth is in prison you give up all control of your life. Today I want to share with you five avenues to take back control of your life by setting and achieving your goals."

3. Statistics:

"*USA Today* reported just this morning that 87 percent of Americans feel that they have lost control of their lives. Eighty-seven percent. I don't have to tell you that's major. That means that forty-seven of you in this room feel lost. Let's see if we can't alter those feelings. If you'll invest the next forty minutes of your attention on the principles I'm about to share, you'll no longer have to be a negative statistic."

4. Question:

"As we get started I want to ask you a question. What is the number one thing that prevents you from living a goal-oriented lifestyle? Think about it a moment. Consider it. Roll it around in your mind.

"OK, how many of you came to the conclusion that the reason you don't have goals is you?

"We are about to take five steps to alleviate that sort of answer."

5. Stunner:

"In the next two minutes I will share a concept about goals that you have never heard and most of you will never attempt. In the next forty minutes I will take that concept and give you five principles for making it a reality in your life."

This is a risky beginning if you don't know the crowd well. They may turn you off immediately if your statement is too strong or too contrary to a deeply held belief.

6. Story:

"About three years ago I woke in a pool of sweat. The doctors called it an anxiety attack. I called it bogus. But the next several months took their toll.

"Like so many other men, I pressed on with little concern for my health or my family. Until February 12. That was the day of the collapse. I was skipping another lunch in an effort to close an important deal that a competitor was hotly pursuing.

"At first my hands began to shake. Then I felt a sharp pain run up my left arm and into my head. That's all I remember until I opened my eyes in the emergency room.

"Long story, short. I overloaded my life with tasks, with events, with work. I knew little of rest, relaxation, or renewal. And certainly balance rarely rose in my vocabulary.

"Maybe you won't reach that extreme. I hope not. But today I am going to share how you can avoid getting near it. A goal-centered life will alleviate unnecessary stress and propel you to greater accomplishment."

7. The Tie-In:

This is a personal favorite. Listen intently to everything that precedes you to hear if anything ties to your topic. If so, use it in your opener. This is one of the strongest openers because it shows you care about their meeting. It also endears you to the crowd because it reveals that you are not scripted.

> "As we get started I want to thank Mr. Logan for his comments about the pace of life that surrounds us. He was right on target when he said that we need to be wiser with our time. In fact, that's the essence of my message tonight. In the next few minutes I'll equip you with five keys to unlock the power of goals. You *will* become more time wise because you will approach each moment with purpose."

8. Relevant News:

"A few minutes before the program I caught a segment on CNN about health. They mentioned that 43 percent of workers are overworked and underpaid. I bet if you surveyed the workers that figure would rise significantly. Who doesn't feel overworked? But is it a reality? Are we really overworked, or under planned?

"Tonight let's pull back the curtain of time and discover how we can tap into the awesome power of goal achieving, and relieve the 'overworked' pressure that flows through us."

9. Twisted Well-Known Quote:

Well known quote: If at first you don't succeed, try, try, again.

Revision: If at first you don't succeed, delegate.

Revision for goal setting: If at first you don't succeed maybe you didn't set a goal.

Step 4: POWER

10. To the Moon:

The moon is a place most have never been. Have you been there? Then tell about it. Anything that the average person has not done takes them to the moon. It's so different they cannot help but be interested.

"Have you seen the Golden Gate Bridge in San Francisco? I used to work on it. The cables that look like strands measure 7,650 feet. They are over three feet in diameter. Thick enough to walk on, to balance on, which is quite easy at the base, but not when the cables begin to stretch toward the towers. That's when wind begins to affect you and you can easily lose sight of your goal: the top. That's when you begin to lose balance.

"The same thing can happen in our lives. When we begin to lose sight of our purpose we begin to lose our bearings. Tonight I'll share the awesome power of achieving goals. These five practical ideas will equip you with the tools you need to set and complete your goals in the areas you want to stretch."

11. Your Own Backyard:

Your own backyard is the place that your entire audience should be familiar with and recognize readily. The strength of the opener comes from getting everyone on your side of the table, or in your boat.

> "Last Saturday my son Steven decided it was time to take the training wheels off his bike. Do you remember your first day without training wheels? Remember the nerves? Remember the fear? But at the same time you were excited, weren't you? We've all been there, right? We all remember when it clicked. When a parent let go and we teetered off. Then we gained more and more balance, and suddenly we could ride. We seemed to glide, didn't we? That's the type of feeling great goals produce. Would you like to wake each day with the excitement of your first bike ride? You can. Tonight I'll show you the awesome power of goal achieving."

The series of "Yes" questions pull people in. Close to 100 percent of the audience will agree with the question and that lets all of us ride together. And that's the way we'll stay until the end of the message.

12. Mystery:

Intrigue works well if you weave it right. It builds suspense and allows the audience to run ahead mentally in an effort to guess the solution.

To use mystery successfully:

- Purposely lead the audience down a wrong path.
- Supply evidence that points where you want it to, but not necessarily to the truth you want revealed later.
- Supply a surprise ending.

"I would like to share five secrets if you don't mind. Secrets not because they're unknown, but unused. But first I would like to tell you an unusual story. A story of a boy, a book, a bowl, and a body."

Five False Starts

Under NO circumstance do you begin your talk with any of the following!

1. The Apology

"I don't why Mrs. Watson asked me to do this. I'm really not a speaker. I want to apologize in advance for my lack of presenting skills."

A common start for beginning speakers, the apology instantly devalues you as a presenter. An apology assumes a mistake. It makes the audience think, "If he's apologizing, why was he invited?"

An apology makes the crowd expect the worst and it will be a tough hole to climb out of if you choose this beginning.

2. The Stare

Another bit of bad advice I received as a beginner was, "Take possession of the platform. Look across the audience and try to look in as many eyes as possible."

That only makes the audience think you're weird. The only time to do it is when you are about to blow them away with an unbelievable opening statement. Other than that, step up to the platform with a smile and a handful of gracious words that move quickly to your opener.

Staring in silence at the audience before your speak not only makes them think you're weird, it also makes them think you've forgotten your talk.

3. The Excuse

A few weeks ago I was speaking to a group that had heard me at several events. I decided to pull out an old message that I knew would be fresh to them. Unfortunately, I left it on my desk and didn't discover it until 30 minutes prior to the meeting.

I knew I was in trouble, *but they didn't*. I asked for a sheet of paper and jotted down as much as I could remember. The session went far better than expected and the crowd never knew the difference.

OK, that's not permission to leave your notes, but it is approval for not making an excuse. Even if the situation warrants it, an excuse makes no one comfortable. It builds listening barriers and makes people think you're irresponsible. (Hey, even if you are irresponsible—like forgetting your notes—the audience never has to know.)

4. The Geek

The geek opening uses jargon familiar only to a few. The geek wants the audience to know his/her I.Q. and tends to use vocabulary as evidence.

If you repudiate to avail yourself of communal manifestation of vocalizations unambiguous to the median stratum of the intimates then you preserve your remarks for geeks like yourself.

5. The Stumble

Shuffling papers, adjusting the microphone, and heaven forbid actually tapping the microphone or saying, "Testing, testing, testing." None of that is appropriate.

Step to the microphone prepared. Have everything in order. If you have questions about the equipment check it out before the meeting.

Now on to the close.

NEVER Close: Reopen

The reopening is more important than the opening. You cannot afford to mess up at this point. Fortunately, if your talk has even been mediocre you can wow the people at this time and send them home thrilled.

Yes, reopening is semantics. But "close" seems so final. You don't want to close the door on the crowd do you? Don't you want to keep their minds open to the thoughts you shared? Don't you want them to keep feeling and not shut off their emotions at your last word?

Irrefutable Law of Speaking

The Reopening Should Create a Feeling of, "I Can't Wait to Hear (Your Name) Again!"

All right, it's *also* supposed to drive the points and purpose deep into the hearts of the audience.

These are the last words heard and first remembered, so make them GREAT!

Six Solid Reopenings

The following examples will continue our speech development. All of these, like the openers, are very abbreviated, but the concept is clear.

1. Emotional

Get the people to feel what you feel. Use a serious as opposed to funny emotional story for the greatest impact.

"Well, we've covered a lot about goal setting and achieving. I wish all would take this advice.

"My father didn't.

"He spent his life floating.

"I don't say this out of bitterness, but reality. The reality of touch.

"Our lives touch the lives of those around us. If we choose to ignore goals in our lives, we choose to make balance impossible for theirs. Choose goals. Not just for yourself, but for everyone."

2. Challenge

Send the crowd out on a dare.

"If you're like most, only 20 percent of you will actually apply this message. Of that 20 percent only 20 percent will continue to apply these concepts six weeks from now. I want to challenge you. You now possess the keys to making the most of each day.

For the next twenty-one days get up thirty minutes earlier than normal. At the end of the day record the differences compared to the previous days when you did not have this insight. Can you do it? Will you invest the next twenty-one days, only ten and a half hours, to goal achieving? The choice is yours. A few days from now your life can be radically changed for the better or depressingly stuck in monotony."

3. Repeat

You never fail when you return to the points and restate them.

"The Awesome Power of a Specific Desire. See what you want to become. Feel what you want to become, specifically.

"The Awesome Power of a Specific Date. Write your goal date on a piece of paper and keep it with you at all times. Look at it several times a day as a reminder.

"The Awesome Power of a Specific Plan. Mark out your plan step by step. Do not leave out a detail. Make it vivid.

"The Awesome Power of a Specific Focus. The number one cause of losing your way is to let it drift away. Stay on target.

"The Awesome Power of a Specific Transformation. Tie your goal to your life so it's not a one-time occurrence but an ongoing victory.

"Live the steps of this message and you will soon *experience* the awesome power of goal achieving."

4. Motivation

Get the group pumped up and believing that what you say is possible.

"On average only 20 percent will actually apply this message. Of that 20 percent only 20 percent will continue to apply these concepts six weeks from now.

"But you're not average are you? If you were you wouldn't be here. As you've listened you've dreamed. You've seen yourself being more productive. You've seen yourself rising early and getting focused. You've seen the results in your mind even as you sat in your chair.

"It's time to take the visuals and make them reality. Resolve right now to achieve. Anyone can write goals on a sheet of paper, but you are different. You will be one of the minority of people who go on to accomplish their dreams. You can. You already know it because you've already seen it!"

5. Recitation

A slightly different version of "repeating" is reciting. Ask the audience to repeat the points with you. You say the point then have them repeat it again with you.

This works well when you have had the audience repeat each point during the talk. That way they already know the points and can repeat them without having to catch on.

"Let's say the points together one more time, and say them LOUD!"

6. Abrupt

Sometimes it's good to come to a stop out of nowhere. The people expect more but you don't give it. You're shockingly finished. This is used so rarely that it does two things:

- The audience will consider you creative if it's done right.
- It causes their minds to repeat your last words in order to form a fitting conclusion. And getting the crowd to think is the best thing you can do.

My friend Joe Donaldson concludes his talks by starting to snap his fingers. I'll use it to illustrate the abrupt close.

Create a soft slow snap in your mind and imagine hearing the following.

"You know, reaching your goals isn't easy, so the sooner you get started the

snap   snap   snap   snap   snap   snap   snap

better. Because life is a lot like this message. When it's over, it's over."

snap   snap   snap   snap   snap   snap   snap

The last "over" and the last snap should happen simultaneously. Then walk off.

That combined snap and "over" will be abrupt, but also produce an "ah-ha" moment in the minds of the audience.

Dos and Don'ts for Reopening

Do Be Tight

This is no time to drift off on a tangent. Write your final remarks down word-for-word. Not so you can memorize it, but so you'll know exactly where you're going.

Make it tight, concrete, and confident.

Don't Add Points

If a new point comes to mind that you think is perfect, wait until the next speech. Give yourself time to develop, design, and deliver the material. Throwing in an impromptu concept without proof and without knowing for sure that it will tie to the purpose can make you look unprepared.

Do Be Clear

If you give instructions, a challenge, or a motivation, make it clear what the people need to do. There's no need to assume that the crowd will be insulted. You don't want to assume that they will get what you're saying even if it's clear to you.

The journalist H.L. Mencken said, "No one in this world, so far as I know . . . has ever lost money by underestimating the intelligence of the great masses of the plain people." There may be some humor in this, but the point is a valid one. You want to make sure that your point is crystal clear and leave no room for doubt in your audience members' minds. There's no need to treat the folks in the seats like idiots, but don't assume they're Edisons either.

An important idea taught in sales training is "Ask for the order." That seems obvious, yet most salesmen don't ask, and most people don't buy.

Your audience will not figure out what to do on their own. Tell them. Clearly.

Don't Return to Forgotten Material

Forgetting a point is fine as long as you don't go back and get it. The people in the seats do not know what you are going to cover unless you have a handout; then they will remind you if you leave something out.

Sharing your fourth point and saying, "Oh, I forgot to mention something on point two, let's backup a minute" makes you look like an amateur.

You might be one, but you don't have to look like one.

Let forgotten material remain forgotten. There will always be points you wish you had hit harder, or stories you'll punch yourself for forgetting. That's how you learn.

Do Conclude

Stop.

Don't keep going if you have nothing to say. The worst thing to do at the end is ramble. It's better to say, "I've got nothing else to say" than to keep talking and prove it.

Don't Go Overtime

Basic rules:

- Ending early hurts no one. If you exit the platform with ten minutes left on the clock, no one will push you back up. But if you stay up for ten minutes after the allotted time, you might get pulled off. A friend of mine who manages large conventions turns off the microphone if the speaker goes long.

- Never acknowledge the time and ignore it. Have you ever heard someone say, "Well, I know I'm supposed to stop about now, but I have a few more things, so hang on"? That statement says the speaker cares more for

Step 4: POWER

himself than the audience. Few people are good enough to go long without consequences.

- Check your watch. If you notice you're over the limit, acknowledge it, apologize, and quickly conclude with your most powerful close.

Step Four in Practice

Paul Evans' Introduction:

> We're grateful to have Paul Evans with us today. Paul is the author of six books including *From the Heart of a Parent*, *Soft Knocks Open Big Doors*, and The *Secret Golf Reports*. As you can tell, Paul has a diversity of interests that allow him to connect to a variety of groups.
>
> Paul is the founder of Evans Communication, through which he created the highly acclaimed Instant Speaking Success System. He works with individuals and businesses not only in communication areas, but also in life value areas. Paul helps people discover their value and purpose both professionally and personally.
>
> He is here today to share "The Awesome Power of Goal Achieving." This message will encourage us to use the five specifics of achievement. If you've ever forsaken a goal, dreamed but dared not attempt, or completed a goal, but found it a shallow victory, you are in for a treat today. Paul will share with us the awesome power of goal achievement.
>
> Please make welcome, Paul Evans!

(You may want to think about your punctuation in the opening. Notice the exclamation point after my name. Hopefully the introducer will pick up on that and punch it. If he does, the audience will feel the anticipation.)

The Awesome Power of Goal Achieving Opening:

Thanks for that great introduction Mike. I even want to hear me!

Well, as Mike revealed we're going to talk about achieving goals, not just setting them. Believe me there's a difference. Anyone can set goals. In fact, 67 percent of American set goals under the guise of resolutions every January. But come February you can interview those same people and only a handful will still be focused on the goals they set only one month before.

Here's how it happens.

A few years ago I owned a fitness center. Every January we knew we would get ten busloads of new members.

(From here I will move into the details of sign up and drop out. Then I'll move to into a "signature story.")

The Awesome Power of Goal Achieving Reopen:

(By this time I've hit all the points and had the audience repeat each one as we went through the message).

Let's go through our achievement specifics one more time. And listen, don't give me some sissy rendition. Shout them out. Put a little energy into it. Going after your goals halfway won't do it.

Here we go.

> *The Awesome Power of a Specific Desire!*
>
> *The Awesome Power of a Specific Date!*
>
> *The Awesome Power of a Specific Plan!*
>
> *The Awesome Power of a Specific Focus!*
>
> *The Awesome Power of a Specific Transformation!*

Awesome!

But it's not enough to shout about it. You've got to do something about it. Let me send you out with a challenge.

But first, two questions.

Thirty days from now will you be forever changed?

Thirty days from now will you be the same?

What you have learned tonight can be applied into a life-altering process. A process that you can repeat over and over again. A process that will cause jaws to drop and knees to knock as they witness the exponential changes taking place in your life.

First, take these specifics and set aside one hour when you get home.

Second, pinpoint one goal you MUST complete in thirty days.

Third, write it on a 3 X 5 card and keep it on you at all times. Review it five times a day.

Fourth, focus and work toward the goal daily.

Thirty days from now will you be forever changed?

Thirty days from now will you be the same?

Step 5
PASSION

"If you can't say it with passion, spare your voice and leave me a note."

- Jeff Walling

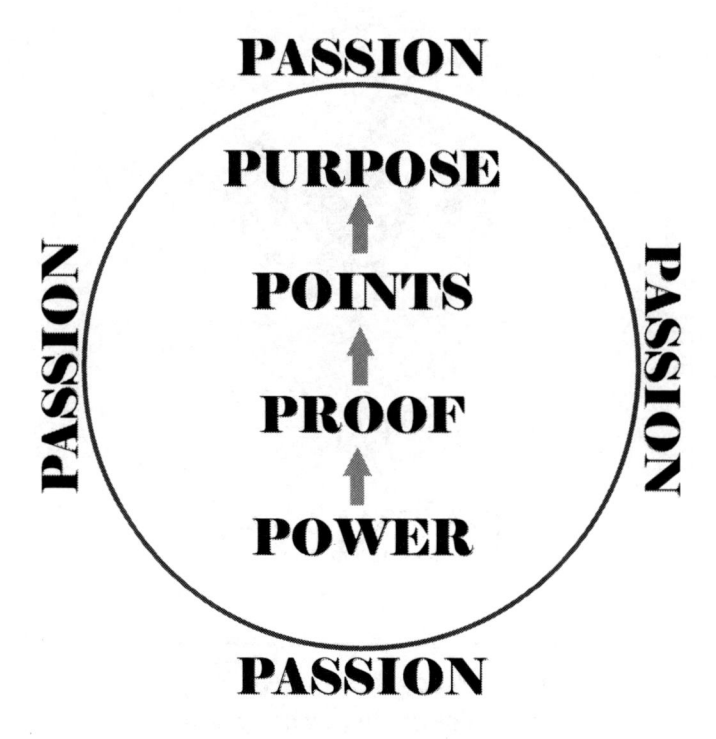

```
            PASSION
          ┌─────────┐
          │ PURPOSE │
          │    ↑    │
  P       │  POINTS │       P
  A       │    ↑    │       A
  S       │  PROOF  │       S
  S       │    ↑    │       S
  I       │  POWER  │       I
  O       └─────────┘       O
  N                         N
            PASSION
```

Your PASSION must engulf your message. Nothing gets into your message without passing through your passion. Nothing gets out of your message without contacting your passion. Period.

Passion cannot be contrived or everyone present can tell it's not authentic.

What is passion to you?

To me it's a state of being. Passion is who you *are*, not what you *do*. With that in mind consider these four Be's when allowing your passion to flow.

Be Real

No one likes a fake. People don't expect you to be perfect. But they do expect you to be real. Presenting yourself as a genuine person will immediately draw the crowd to you.

What is real? Well, it allows people to receive what they see. It means that what you say and do match.

When people come to hear a speaker they're hoping for two things. First, they want valuable information that they can apply to their personal lives. Second, they want to know that the speaker lives what he says. We like to hear an authority, but we LOVE to hear a person who has experienced what he or she is talking about.

A lady who used to weigh 350 pounds, but now weighs 150 pounds, has much more credibility speaking about weight loss than one who has always weighed 150 pounds.

When the audience "sees" where we are now compared to where we were it gives them hope. If *we* can do it they believe *they* can do it.

Be Confident

Confidence comes from knowing the audience, knowing the material, and knowing your real ability. The crowd loves a confident speaker.

Arrogance comes from thinking you're superior to the audience, with a superior message that no one else can match, and the belief you have gifts no one else can touch. Since you bought this book, I seriously doubt you feel any of that, but it could develop as you get better and better.

Confident humility is critical for a speaker who wants to have a lasting impact. Walk to the platform and appear comfortable. A comfortable look alone may keep the audience's attention for thirty or forty minutes, even if your material is weak.

Comedian John Cantu says, "Even though you don't feel like a great speaker, the audience will perceive you as a much stronger speaker because you are on the platform—and they are the audience. They respect that."

Be Valuable

Provide the following three things in every message and you cannot fail even if you don't feel that you did your best.

1. Equip

Fill your message with equipping content. The people should walk out with practical points they can immediately apply to make their lives better. Don't just tell them what to do, tell them **how** to do it.

Equipping means you put the tools and resources in the hands of the audience members, so they can become your message.

What speaker have you heard lately that equipped you? What equipping principles did you learn?

2. Encourage

You want people to leave motivated. They need to believe that what you spoke about can be a reality in their lives. If you're speaking on goals, they should see themselves setting and reaching those goals. If you're speaking on raising money for a children's hospital, they should see the children that will be healed because of their contributions.

Fill each person with hope and faith. Help them see themselves achieving the end result of your speech. Encourage them to keep going when they want to quit. Help them recognize the winning attitudes that must be in place in their lives.

In what ways has a speaker encouraged you? What lines or phrases can you remember that made you think, "Yeah, I can do that"?

3. Entertain

This doesn't mean you have to be funny—though it doesn't hurt. It means you keep the audience's attention. They will want to hear you again after you're finished. You don't have to be flawless, but you do need to be engaging.

You entertain by using interesting proof—stories, illustrations, and examples that keep the people focused on the points and purpose.

What was entertaining about a talk you heard?

Consider those three Es for every speaker you hear. Write down the specific ways equipping, encouragement, and entertainment come to you. Then think about the ways you can use the same concepts in your talks.

I guarantee those three Es wherever I speak. The people expect it, and it's my responsibility to provide it.

Be Excited

Be excited instead of intimidated that you were invited to speak.

Be excited that the one who offered you the opportunity thought enough of you to do so.

Be excited that the people in the seats will soon gain life-altering knowledge.

Be excited that you may get an unexpected "thank you" from a person who applies your message.

Write your own reasons for being excited:

Be excited_____.

Be excited_____.

Be excited_____.

Be excited_____.

Be excited_____.

It is an honor to be invited to speak. It means the people believe you have something to share of importance. It means they believe in your character. It means they believe you will do a good job, even if you don't believe.

Irrefutable Law of Speaking

YOU are the Message.

Step 6
PERIMETERS

Beginning speakers get overwhelmed with gestures, voice, etc. Don't put too much into it, right now these are just perimeters—the outside edge of your talk. Get your message down first.

The following concepts are all you need at this point. You can get training on any aspect if you feel it's critical. But unless you're making $1,000 and up per speech there's no real need to let any of the following get to you emotionally.

Voice

Your voice is the delivery system. It takes words and gives them texture and emotion.

How do you speak to a friend? How do you sound when you tell someone about your new car? About a movie you saw? About your job? About your relationships? About your kids?

Irrefutable Law of Speaking
*Use **YOUR** Voice – Don't Speak Monotone.*

That's the only thing you must master.

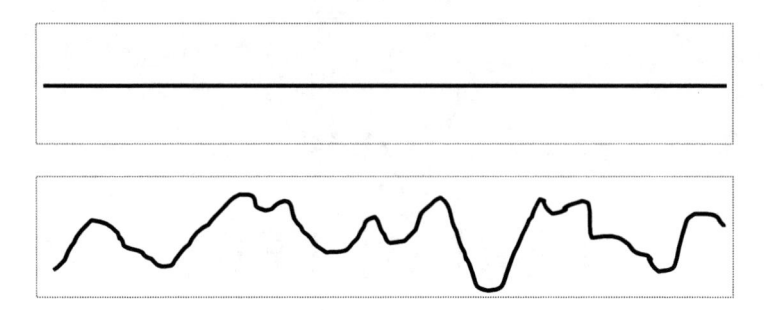

In the graphs above think of the straight line as perfect monotone. The squiggly line a vocal variance. You want to be squiggly. Give your voice rhythm and variation.

Become a Vocal Magnet…

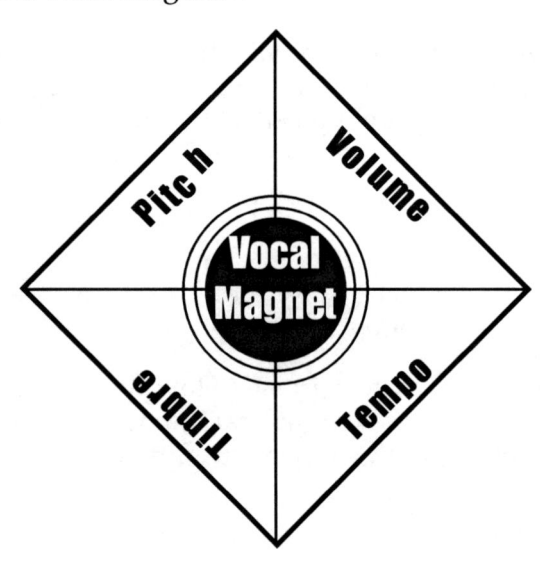

- **Pitch** refers to how high and low you speak. Present with a variety of range.

- **Volume** conveys intensity and emotion. Use everything from a shout to a whisper.

- **Tempo** suggests speed. Let your feelings determine your speed. The more animated you are, the faster you talk—the less enthusiastic, the more slowly you speak.

- **Timbre** speaks to the resonance or tone of your voice. Strive for a clear quality understood by all present.

The combination of those four forms a vocal magnet. The crowd will be drawn to you.

Let these items happen naturally.

1. Whisper when you tell critical information.

2. Let your volume rise and fall according to the mood at that section of the message.

3. Vary your pitch. When you talk about something that excites you let your pitch go higher. When you want to create drama let your voice fill to a lower tone.

4. Eliminate dead words. Uh, um, and the like have no place in a speech unless you are illustrating how not to speak.

5. Do not be afraid of silence. Pausing in a message gives the audience time to reflect, while giving you a chance to think.

6. Vary your rhythm and pace. Speak faster when excited. Slower when trying to be precise or wanting to emphasize.

7. Audio tape yourself in the car practicing different sections of your talk. Review it and do it again the next day until it sounds natural.

8. Talk to yourself—a lot—using diverse dynamics. Try to sound angry. Try to sound sad. Try to sound happy. Try to imitate a voice.

Gestures

Like everything else in speaking, your gestures should be natural. Don't do as one speaker I saw who said, "Then Moses when up on the mountain." He stalled and then pointed up. "Then he came down." He stopped again and pointed to the floor.

Do:

- Become aware of how you use your body during average conversations.

- Become conscious of your motions without becoming self-conscious.

- Think fluid and flowing.

- Watch other speakers and notice their movement. Write down anything you learn and seek ways to apply it.

- Pick up on a presenter's poor gestures and determine why you don't want to repeat them.

- Watch your video tape and see if you can strengthen your gestures, or if a certain movement is repeated too often.

- Relax.

- Be natural

Don't:

- Speak with your arms crossed, hands in your pockets, or gripping the podium for long periods.

- Wonder what to do with your hands, let it happen.

- Choreograph gestures.

- Jingle change in your pocket, constantly adjust glasses, or any other mannerisms that distract.

Attire

Dress for the occasion. A general rule says dress one level above the audience. I say ask the person who invited you what to wear, and *ask specifically*.

No-brainer advice:

- Arrive wrinkle free. When the engagement will require a flight or a several hour drive, take your clothes separately and change. There's no excuse for looking like a mess.

- Look sharp. Wear colors that complement, not ones that distract.

- Match your message. Don't dress like a clown unless you are one.

- Look professional, but not stuffy.

- Talk to a friend whose style you admire. Some people just know how to dress. Get their advice.

The Eyes Have It!

We do not trust people who will not look at us in the eyes. We think they are hiding something (who knows, they might be!).

Eye contact communicates care and intimacy. The main reason we don't maintain it well is insecurity and being intimidated by the person with whom we are speaking. Insecure because we're afraid they may notice we're afraid. Intimidated because we think the person might not agree with us, or might think we're a novice, or naive, or dumb.

General speaking advice states: Look at portions of the room; look at the tops of the audience's heads; graze the crowd in each direction. It's a lot easier and a lot more profitable just to look into a person's eyes than follow any of that former advice.

You will not be able to look into every eye in the crowd, but hit as many as possible.

Reasons to look into the audience's eyes:

- It builds rapport.
- It says, "You can trust me."
- It creates the feeling of conversation verses presentation.
- Coupled with a smile it overcomes a multitude of speaking mistakes.
- It increases attention. "Look into my eyes, you're not getting sleepy."
- It helps you focus.
- It lets the people in the seats know that you are interested in them.

Room Dynamics

Few perfect speaking rooms exist. Sound systems squeal. Noisy chairs make noise during the talk. Some acoustics create a Grand Canyon echo. Projection systems fail. The power goes off. People wander in from the street.

What does all that have to do with your message? Very little.

Books have been written on how to set a room up properly to make a speech the most powerful. Personally I don't think it matters too much. If anything a poor setup makes the audience pay more attention. They are afraid of missing something good.

When you're speaking to thousands get a little more concerned about room dynamics. Until then, do three things:

1. Make sure the microphone works and is easily adjustable to your height. Do not fidget with it when you get up to speak. Better yet, wear a wireless microphone and make sure you know how to turn it on.

2. Make sure all the chairs face you.

3. Check any presentation equipment before the meeting to make sure it works properly.

Just-in-Case Planning

Sometimes things just don't go as planned. Do you have a contingency plan?

Here's THE answer. Make sure your talk is strong enough to survive the video failing, the PowerPoint going out, props getting damaged, etc. You've probably noticed that I don't cover multimedia or props even though they're great tools. Maybe I'll go into detail in a later course about those items, but the point remains.

Your message should not be dependant on extras. You should be all it needs.

Step 7
PRACTICE

These techniques and concepts will help you deliver a message with maximum impact and minimal effort.

First, I want to remind you again that the audience has no idea what you are presenting. They will not know if you said everything you planned or if you left something out. They won't know that you forgot your favorite illustration.

Second, too much practice will cause you exaggerated anxiety because you will panic when you don't say what you practiced. You don't practice a conversation at the water cooler, do you? If you did, you might flub it.

Third, I want to encourage you to trust yourself. If you can carry on a discussion with any other human on the planet and keep their attention, you can become a great speaker with the smallest amount of practice.

Delivery Options

When a lady has a child there are primarily three delivery options—yes, they'll relate to speaking.

First, natural childbirth. This is the most painful and the most bragged about. Many ladies (not all) who give birth naturally—without painkillers of any form or fashion—love to tell others about the wonderful experience and they'll say that this is the only *true* way to give birth.

Second, Cesarean section births. This is not the desired delivery option. My youngest was a C-section baby, and I can tell you from being there, it's not the best route. It's more painful, takes longer to recuperate, and leaves scars.

Third, epidural delivery. Drug-enhanced childbirth. It's still work, but much easier and less painful than the other two options.

Let's correlate these delivery styles to our subject.

1. Speaking without Notes

The natural childbirth option of the speaking world. Speakers who don't use notes want others to know. Beginners often look at such people with awe. "If only I could speak without notes."

It might look good, but it's not all it's cracked up to be. If all doesn't go right it's painful, even embarrassing. Speaking without notes is not worth the risk compared to the reward.

My personal advice—don't do it. The audience doesn't notice the difference in a speaker who uses notes and those who don't.

2. Reading a Manuscript

The speaking equivalent of a cesarean section: painful, long healing time, and leaves scars.

Step 7: PRACTICE

Painful to the listeners. If they wanted to be read to they could go to story hour at the local bookstore. People who read a manuscript want to be sure they say everything they planned to say. But since no one will be paying attention it won't matter.

Long time healing because the person who reads can tell afterward that audience reception is cold.

Leaves scars because the reader will begin to doubt his/her actual speaking ability.

My personal advice—don't do it.

3. Notes

Notes compare to an epidural delivery. Sure there's pain involved, but nothing like it would be without a painkiller.

No audience cares if a speaker uses notes. Just use them as light reminders to jog your memory. That way you can keep your focus on the people and not your paper.

The Step Four in Practice section will give you a good outline form to use. Some people like to put different points on 3 x 5 cards, but I like to keep it all on one sheet so I don't have to turn any pages. Another option is to get some half-sheet sticky paper and put it on the lectern. You don't have to be concerned about it blowing off.

Three Rs of Being Memorable

By choosing a structure that makes your points memorable you make it easier for you to remember, and you make it easier for the audience to remember. But here's some extra insurance to keep your information anchored in their minds.

Repeating

When you make a point ask the audience to repeat it after you.

139

"Number 1: The Awesome Power of a Specific Desire. Now say that with me. The Awesome Power of a Specific Desire. One more time."

With each additional point ask the crowd to repeat the previous points.

"Quick reviews. Point one was . . . good. Point two . . . Point three . . . excellent. Now point four is The Awesome Power of a Specific Focus. Say that with me."

Reading

Use overheads or presentation equipment when possible. It allows the group to visually and audibly connect. Ask the audience to read each point out loud with you.

Reading your message makes you boring. Asking the audience to read with you makes you relational.

(W)riting

Provide an outline. You might think that a fill-in-the-blank format is too immature, but people like to go home with stuff. At least tell the people present to write down the information. Although the idea with this course is for you to design unforgettable messages it doesn't hurt if people take notes.

How To Practice:

In order of ease:

1. Practice sections of your speech on your friends.

    - Don't tell them.

    - Use your opener or close on a friend as part of a casual conversation and judge their reaction. Does she laugh? Is he intrigued?

- Whenever a discussion goes anywhere near one of your points use your point as an opinion. Then back it up with some of the proof you've uncovered.

2. Drive yourself crazy.

    - Turn off the cell phone and talk to yourself in the car.

    - Really let it rip in your vehicle. Shout if you want. Get soft. Use extreme vocal ranges.

    - Go over portions of your talk again and again.

    - Let a stream of consciousness flow through you. Don't worry about perfection. Have fun.

3. Find an empty room and talk to the walls.

    - Do not be concerned with perfection. What is "right" anyway?

    - Be conversational. Talk as you would to a friend.

    - Have fun and be as crazy as you want.

    - Exaggerate your tones and gestures.

    - Smile

4. Video Tape Yourself.

    - Follow the tips in the first point.

    - Pretend the camera is the audience and see how much eye contact you keep.

    - As you watch the tape count the number of dead words (ah, um, uh, etc.).

- Do not be too critical. Take a casual approach.
- Yes, that is your real voice. No, it's not as bad as you think.

5. Ask your friends over and videotape the message.
    - Follow the first two tips.
    - Get ten to twenty friends in a room.
    - Make eye contact with each person at some point during the talk.
    - Pretend only one person is there and that you are talking only to him or her as you would over a casual dinner.

6. Speak for free everywhere you can.
    - By taking any opportunity to speak you can get a lot of practice in for free.
    - You can take the same message to a variety of groups.
    - It's as easy as calling some local civic groups (Kwanis, Rotary, etc.) and saying, "I'm a local speaker who would like to speak to your group sometime on _____."

Another valuable option is joining an organization such as Toastmasters International (www.toastmasters.org).

Toastmasters will teach you basic speaking skills and give you the opportunity to get positive feedback and critiques.

The more you practice the more comfortable you will become and the less fear you will experience.

Irrefutable Law of Speaking
Have a Conversation with the Audience.

As you practice, make conversation a goal. THERE IS NO OTHER ASPECT OF SPEAKING THAT IS MORE IMPORTANT. If you can learn to talk to a crowd as you talk to a friend over dinner, you'll be a hit. This cannot be over emphasized.

A speaker who sounds like a speaker rarely gets the full attention of the crowd. But when you connect you'll hear things like, "I felt like you were talking just to me." What does that mean? You were conversational.

A breakthrough moment in my speaking came when a friend said this after a presentation, "That was you tonight. You didn't act like a speaker. Your voice didn't change. You were the same on stage as right now."

Speak *with* the audience not *to* the audience.

Secrets of an average conversation that you must take to the platform:

- A natural voice gets excited, gets sad, gets angry, gets happy, gets emotional.
- Use natural gestures. I've never known anyone to stop talking at the dinner table and say, "Wow! Did you catch that gesture? It went right with what I was telling you." Instead, conversational gestures just happen.

Get BIG. Most people get small on stage. Their voices, gestures, confidence, knowledge, expertise, all shrink on stage.

Don't try to be a speaker; be YOU.

PUTTING IT ALL TOGETHER

Here's the message we've been working on. Below you have an example of what I would walk on stage with.

Paul Evans' Introduction: (read by Mike)

Opening: Thank Mike. Goals

The Awesome Power of a Specific Desire

1. What do you want more than anything? Be specific.

2. How to write down everything you've ever wanted

3. How to make it specific

4. Why clarity is paramount – *USA Today* article

5. 97 percent never set goals.

The Awesome Power of a Specific Date

1. Read section from *7 Habits*

2. Funny wedding story about setting "the date"
3. How to determine what date to set

   Amount of planning

   Amount of effort
4. Quote Zig Ziglar in *Over the Top*
5. The great calendar countdown technique.

The Awesome Power of a Specific Plan

1. Joke about father and son in park
2. Story about my forgetting my glasses
3. Jerusalem's walls in 52 days

   Workers, Guards, Opposition, Victory

The Awesome Power of a Specific Focus

1. Why vivid descriptions beat generic ones. Psychology magazine pg 82
2. The power of autosuggestion by Napoleon Hill
3. How to block distractions

   Breakthrough

   Build up

The Awesome Power of a Specific Transformation

1. Tie your goal to life
2. One time success or lifetime triumph?
3. How Walt Disney changed us forever

4. Pinpointing your specific transformation

   Need

   Desire

   Impact

Reopen: Repeat points with audience. Thirty-day challenge.

Thirty days from now will you be forever changed?

Thirty days from now will you be forever the same?

How to Get the Most from the Following Worksheets

1. Copy the sheets and use them for each presentation.
2. Copy one Points Worksheet for EACH point you will make in your message.
3. Don't take shortcuts.

Purpose Worksheet

Meeting Contact: _____

Event Name: _____

Reason for Event: _____

The Messages...

Narrow Topic:_____

Head: _____

Heart: _____

PURPOSE (the sum of everything you want to say. Every point, proof, power, perimeter, and passion MUST lead back to the purpose.)

_____

_____

Title of the Message: _____

Points Worksheet

(choose a structure)

Points Discovered From Research: (List every point you want to use in your message).

_____

_____

_____

_____

_____

Point Structure: (check one).

- ❑ Acrostic
- ❑ Alpha-Series
- ❑ Rhyme
- ❑ Phrase
- ❑ Analogy

Convert Your POINTS into the Chosen Structure:

_____

_____

_____

_____

Proof Worksheet

(Duplicate this sheet for EACH point.
Log PROOF sources next to the category.)

Point # _____ : _____

❏ Life	❏ Analogies
❏ Quotes	❏ Interviews
❏ News	❏ Statistics
❏ Newspapers	❏ Stories
❏ Movies	❏ Definitions
❏ Songs	❏ Examples
❏ Poetry	❏ Syndicated Columns
❏ Books	❏ Television
❏ Conversations	❏ Jokes
❏ Benches	❏ Success Stories
❏ Bumper Stickers	❏ The Bible
❏ Magazines	❏ Everywhere!
❏ Ezines	

Power Opening Worksheet

(Choose ONE of the following OPENING styles.)

❏ Quote	❏ The Tie-In
❏ Joke	❏ Relevant News
❏ Statistic	❏ Twisted Quote
❏ Question	❏ To the Moon
❏ Shocker	❏ Your Backyard
❏ Story	❏ Mystery

Write out your opening based on the selected style…

_____

_____

_____

_____

_____

_____

_____

_____

_____

_____

_____

_____

Power Reopen Worksheet

(Choose ONE of the following CLOSING styles.)

☐ Emotional	☐ Motivation
☐ Challenge	☐ Recitation
☐ Repeat	☐ Abrupt

Write out your close based on the selected style...

_____
_____
_____
_____
_____
_____
_____
_____
_____
_____
_____
_____
_____
_____

Passion Worksheet

Be Real

How is this message revealed through your life?

_____

_____

Be Confident

Why are you THE person to deliver this message?

_____

_____

Be Valuable

How will the audience be changed as a result of this message?

_____

_____

Be Excited

What excites you most about the opportunity to share this topic?

_____

_____

Your words are powerful and transforming.

Construct them carefully.

Use them wisely.

Refer to this resource regularly to build strong messages of massive value. But this is just the beginning. Continue to grow and learn.

I hope we can continue this speaking relationship. More resources are being developed to help you become the best speaker you can be.

Thank you.

For caring about your audience enough to give them the best.

For caring about yourself enough to get focused and get good.

Your Public Speaking Coach,

Paul

About the Author

Paul Evans is the founder of Evans Communication and Consulting. Each year he speaks to thousands on the critical topics of communication and life value.

Paul is the author of six books, each focusing on changing people and business for good. His conversational style engages audiences the world over by challenging them to achieve more than they ever thought possible.

Paul supports and is active in the work of 100X Missions whose mission is to rescue and redeem orphans. 100% of all gifts to 100X go directly to the children. No overhead or expenses are extracted. Visit 100XMissions.org for more information.

Learn More from Paul

InstantSpeakingSuccess.com

Get Free Training and Communication Strategies

PaulBEvans.com

When you're losing the crowd.

You may not believe this (in fact you probably won't)

Lets pull over for a moment

Lets back that up... (Recap)

I probably shouldn't say this
     (I was talking to ... and /p.s.s.this)

Ok, look at you notes. Tell me one thing that you've learned so far.